The Counselling of Couples in Healthcare Settings

A Handbook for Clinicians

PATRICIA D'ARDENNE PsychD

Barts and the London School of Medicine and
East London and The City Mental Health NHS Trust

and

DEIRDRE MORROD MB, ChB

One Plus One, Marriage and Partnership Research

W

WHURR PUBLISHERS
LONDON AND PHILADELPHIA

© 2003 Whurr Publishers Ltd
First published 2003
by Whurr Publishers Ltd
19b Compton Terrace
London N1 2UN England and
325 Chestnut Street, Philadelphia PA 19106 USA

British Library Cataloguing in Publication Data

A catalogue record for this book
is available from the British Library.

ISBN 1 86156 360 4

Typeset by Adrian McLaughlin, a@microguides.net
Printed and bound in the UK by Athenæum Press Ltd, Gateshead,
Tyne & Wear.

Contents

For our parents
Dennis and Biddy d'Ardenne and Ben and Kay Sherlock

Foreword

One of the hardest things to do when a marriage or partnership is under pressure is to ask for help – from a partner, from friends, from family members, and certainly from counsellors and therapists. It's relatively OK to seek help for oneself, and even for problems that surface between parents and children, but to confide in others about couple and sexual problems can be shaming in the extreme. Breaking a boundary of privacy can feel deeply disloyal, however problematic a relationship has become. The fear of exposure, of subsequent conflict, of humiliation, and even of separation, can be sufficient to drive everything underground. Small wonder, then, that the private pain of relationship distress can be referred through the body and find expression in physical symptoms of one kind or another. Those working in the health field will be most aware of how tightly wed are psyche and soma, and how the language of illness is often used as an acceptable tongue for communicating about ailments that are less easily put into words.

Psychosomatic-cum-relationship dis-ease is just part of the jigsaw facing those delivering services in the health sector. What about the consequences for couples of serious illness in either partner or their children? What implications might follow from a shift in the balance of care in the partnership? How will new parents decide who is to look after whom when a young baby devours the bank of their caring resources and more? Is tact and diplomacy a sufficient response when sexual health problems threaten intimacy in a relationship?

As difficult as the patient's dilemma of disclosure can be, so is the practitioner's dilemma of response. When she or he senses that there is a missing dimension to the presenting symptom should the supplementary question be asked or not? And if it is, what can of worms might be opened up? If there is even a whiff of a relationship problem what possible reason can there be for health practitioners to venture out of role into the privacy of the conjugal bedroom? How easy it can be for a collusive alliance to be forged between patient and practitioner, in which the former only half tells and the latter only half listens, with the consequence that the presenting problem must stubbornly persist in ambivalently drawing attention to something bigger than itself.

What is evident from the compact treasure trove of research evidence, clinical vignette and practical guidance contained in this book, is how intricately connected are health issues and the quality of adult partnerships. The evidence is that good partnerships have positive health effects, and when ill health prevails there is a vital social dimension to the recovery process – as well as the management of conditions from which there can be no recovery. While we have come to accept that having parents involved in the hospital care of their children is of immense value to both parties, we have been slower to see that the same logic applies to adults. So the message is: it helps to keep a patient's partner in mind when planning treatment.

Health practitioners have enormous potential to make a difference to the lives and loves of their patients by simply recognizing that many of them will be in partnerships, and by considering the implications. These partnerships represent a frequently untapped resource that can be harnessed to the therapeutic endeavour. This is not to say that everyone must be a couple counsellor – that would plainly be absurd and inappropriate – but it is to affirm that the art of listening is at the heart of all good therapeutic practice, whatever the professional role of the practitioner.

The purpose of this book, made explicit by the authors from the outset, is to build an awareness of the potential gains that can follow from those working in health settings taking the intimate relationships of their patients into account, and to boost their confidence in doing so. It is apparent that health professionals are regularly exposed to the relationship problems of their patients and challenged to make a response. Individual responses are very different, but simply acknowledging the issues raised indirectly by those seeking help can make a significant difference, and can mobilize the resources of patients and their partners. The health professional's knowledge of what resources are available for more specialist help, and the way that she or he uses it, can also make a big difference to the lives of couples.

So this is an important book. It acts not only as a reminder that the Cartesian split between body and mind is – or, at least, should be – a thing of the past, but also that illness is a social matter: ailments are both socially defined and have social consequences, especially for committed adult partnerships. In our quest to treat people as people, to be holistic in our thinking about what makes for health and illness, this book is as useful as it is timely. Practitioners will identify with the dilemmas of response contained in the case illustrations, and will find something of practical value in the summary of do's and don'ts contained at the end of each chapter. I commend it to you warmly.

Christopher Clulow
Tavistock Marital Studies Institute, London.
February, 2003.

Acknowledgements

Our trainees and patient couples and the many health professionals we have worked with served as our inspiration and primary focus while we were preparing this book, and we extend our thanks to them for everything they have shared with us.

We are grateful for the ongoing support and encouragement from the staff of One Plus One, Marriage and Partnership Research, and we extend particular thanks to its director, Penny Mansfield, to Joy Read for her willingness and skill in researches, and to Jim Wallman for IT support.

The Resource List owes much to the perseverance and good humour of Peter Kenyon, although we own all errors in content and form.

We have been fortunate in receiving feedback and ideas from our colleagues, and would like to mention in particular Maggie Rose.

Our thanks go to the editorial team at Whurr for their professionalism, patience and belief in the project.

Lastly, this book would not have been possible without the loving help of our own husbands, Peter and Rod, who provided practical and moral support throughout.

CHAPTER 1

Introduction

Background

This book was inspired by the clinicians we train and supervise. They meet couples daily in their clinical practice and want to help them use their relationship more creatively for health maintenance and education, compliance with treatment and improved communication. The clinicians described struggling with a lack of confidence in their skill in engaging both partners in the task of returning to health. They also acknowledged the difficulties of dealing with intrusive, subversive and even aggressive partners, as well as in knowing how and when to refer troubled couples on to a relevant counsellor or therapist. They expressed a wish for a basic handbook on good practice for professionals working with couples in healthcare settings.

Many clinicians do not see themselves as working with couples. Our health training is focused on care of the individual patient. Western medical models and nomenclature place people as patients within a biological rather than a psychosocial framework. It is little wonder then that, faced with a couple in the above setting, the clinician may feel anxious and out of depth. However, we are aware of staff who want to work with the couple, or even the whole family, but who feel ill trained, unsupported and always pressed for time. It requires a significant cultural shift for the health professional to take the further step of engaging the patient's partner in the process of a health pact. For the needs of the couple to be met and the opportunity they present to be used, the practitioner has to include the partner and plan interventions in a very different way. We hope that this book will be part of that cultural shift and will help the reader help the couple and increase effectiveness with them. You may come to see partners as potential allies whose presence will help patients with communication, motivation, choices and sharing the journey through the illness.

We were motivated by the idea of clinicians forming an alliance with both patient and partner to improve health and wellbeing. We are aware of the extensive literature in the field of couple relationships and human sexuality (Hawton 1985; Bancroft 1989), some of it placed within the context of health, but much of it less accessible to the busy clinician. However, a basic handbook still eluded us. Our response to our trainees is this book, which we hope will have a wider interest.

We want this book to help build the confidence of any clinician facing couples in health settings and to raise awareness of what can be achieved for health gain within the context of the strengths and weaknesses of an intimate relationship. There is a body of evidence that shows that committed partnerships correlate significantly with physical and mental wellbeing (McAllister 1995). We regard the couple relationship as a resource that is neglected and hope this book will help generate more creative solutions to family healthcare problems.

Models used

Our model of the couple is based on the idea of a committed sexual relationship, whether married or unmarried, heterosexual or homosexual, living together or separately, and with or without religious sanction. Implicit in this book is that our patient is the one who is ill, but there will be many clinical instances when both partners are affected by an illness or condition, either by choice or by chance. Our model of illness, therefore, is that it is a biological, social and interpersonal experience. It is this shared experience that we wish to tap into, and help the practitioner use for clinical gain.

It is not our intention to train readers to become marital and sexual therapists. We hope readers will recognise personal and professional boundaries with the couple, as well as when and how to refer them on to specialist support. Not all relationships are supportive or even accessible to change. Clinicians also need to decide when not to get involved with the partner. Our aim is to expand the range of responses available to the clinician treating the patient.

Engaging with partners is valuable because they may be the first to recognise that there is a health problem and will initiate the search for help. The partner is able to provide the clinician with vital information about the patient's health status, history, medication and behaviour. The partner may be involved in decision-making, consent-giving and mediating between all parties. Partners may be required to undertake a substantial and immediate change of role and be expected to provide ongoing emotional, physical and financial support to the patient. Lastly, the partner may be needed to monitor health and encourage and even organise treatment compliance.

Working with couples, whether in psychotherapy or in counselling, is about emotional engagement and offering them a secure base from which to explore feeling (Clulow 2001). It is also about providing an opportunity for couples to identify and deal with their problems and make more careful decisions, some of which will have a direct impact on their health. In some cases, for example, an individual's health may be helped by his or her decision to separate.

A word about ourselves

Our backgrounds are complementary – we both help professionals with couples, but in different ways. Deirdre Morrod is a physician and Head of Practice Development at One Plus One, a national marriage and partnership research organisation. She has a background in obstetrics, gynaecology and mental health, and is responsible for creating and developing training courses and materials for health professionals and the public, including couples. She has devised the *Brief Encounters* training course (Morrod 2002), which is designed to give health professionals and others working with families the skills and confidence to deal with relationship problems. She has also worked with lawyers, teachers, clergy and social care professionals. She has had many years' clinical experience as a marital and sexual counsellor, for both a local health authority and for Marriage Care, a UK national marriage counselling organisation.

Patricia d'Ardenne is an NHS clinical psychologist and psychotherapist, who works with people with sexual and relationship difficulties and who supervises health professionals who work with distressed couples. She has experience in mental health, sexual health and primary care in the UK, Europe and US. She directs an East London psychotrauma unit and works in a community mental health team. She was Editor-in-Chief of *Sexual and Marital Therapy*, the journal of the Association for Sexual Relationship Therapy (published by Bruner-Routledge) and has written widely on cross-cultural counselling and relationship disorders.

On a personal note

This book was written at a time when we were balancing the competing demands of our work, our frail parents, our children, our grandchildren, and our partners. We consequently recognise the immense value of clinicians who are aware of, and caring enough, to consider patients in their family setting.

A word about language

This book is about couples in intimate and committed relationships. This includes not only traditional marriages, but also couples living together, including same-sex relationships, visiting relationships and other less conventional family patterns which reflect the diversity of our current world.

Our model for couples includes all those partners affected 'for better or worse' by their 'significant other'. Mansfield and Collard (1988) describe the recent changes in modern domestic arrangements and explore the reasons why couples now choose alternative partnerships. We use the term 'married' or 'spouse' only where it describes such a relationship, but we recognise that the term 'partner' is loose and not always an adequate description of the most important person in one's life. We have had to balance the needs of inclusion with the inadequacies of language. When we have had to refer to a specific clinician, we have used the pronoun 'she', for simplicity and clarity.

Why partnerships in health?

Much of the initial work on linking committed relationships to health and wellbeing was inspired by Dr Jack Dominian (1995), the founder of One Plus One, Marriage and Partnership Research (formerly the Marriage Research Centre). The development of that work led to training and working in partnership with health professionals. In a study by One Plus One, Marriage and Partnership Research (Ayles and Reynolds 2001), health professionals in a West Midlands Health Authority were interviewed in depth about how they identified relationship problems, how they were disclosed and how they were managed. The study looked in particular at referral to counselling services and made the following key findings:

- Health professionals were regularly exposed to patients' relationship problems. However, these types of difficulties were not addressed routinely or systematically, and often would not be revealed by patients for some time. Health professionals did not see relationship problems as a *core concern* (our emphasis).
- The response to relationship difficulties depended largely on the individual health professional. Most felt comfortable containing minor problems, but there was concern and anxiety about what to do in more serious cases.
- Few direct referrals were made to counsellors. More commonly, health professionals suggested to patients that they should contact counselling services, most usually Relate (formerly the National Marriage Guidance Council).
- Knowledge of local counselling services and the methods and qualifications of counsellors was very limited and usually obtained

unsystematically. Most health professionals would like more information. The provision of additional skills and information might allow health professionals to respond to relationship distress more effectively.

- There was very little contact between health professionals and counsellors. Health professionals rarely knew whether patients had taken up counselling or the outcome of any attendance. Counsellors were generally wary of having contact with health professionals for reasons of confidentiality. Both parties would generally prefer greater collaboration.
- The study also showed that health professionals understood very clearly the prevalence of relationship problems and their impact on mental and physical health.

Layout and chapters

The book is organised loosely around lifecycle developmental stages within healthcare contexts. We start with counselling skills that are common to engaging couples in any healthcare setting. Each chapter is divided into an introduction, history, rationale, clinical settings, type of couple problems, case examples and guidelines for good practice. We were also motivated to help the reader understand when to refer couples in trouble to specialist services and when to stay with the couple. We have devoted the last chapter to this issue, reflecting our belief that health professionals are often the first people to whom couples will reveal distress or dysfunction. Health crises expose the strengths and weaknesses of a relationship and provide an important time for couples to decide to seek further help with their relationship. Lastly, we provide a resource section for those who want to encourage their patients in a more holistic and empowering way. We have selected cases and chapter headings that address these themes.

Settings

We recognise that health settings for couples can occur in hospitals, specialist units, in the community or in the couple's own home, and there will be many connections between the chapters. It is hoped that readers who work predominantly in one care setting will be interested in considering couples in other services or at other stages of the lifecycle and will recognise some common themes throughout. Some couple issues apply regardless of the healthcare setting in which they occur and we have attempted to introduce these as often as possible. These include sexuality and intimacy, violence and the management of risk. We are aware that these issues are a major source of anxiety with any clinician. Readers are advised to use the index to establish where these themes re-emerge.

Further work

Books are often the beginning of a journey and we are pleased to provide students and readers with resources that we and our colleagues have found useful. We include a list of organisations concerned with the welfare of the couple, as well as a list of recommended reading, which will be up to date at the time of going to press, and will represent a starting point for those who want to build on their knowledge base. The references are inclusive of all our resource texts, and we hope that readers will be encouraged to explore these further for themselves. We also hope that by introducing good practice at the end of each chapter, readers will have the opportunity to revise the key messages from the text and that they will identify practical and positive ways forward with their existing clinical dilemmas.

Readership

This book is aimed at any health professional who comes into contact with the patient and partner, as well as those who train and supervise them. We include nurses and physicians, especially general practitioners, district nurses, health visitors, midwives, physiotherapists, occupational therapists, health advisors, clinical nurse specialists, health advocates, clinical and counselling psychologists, counsellors and psychotherapists. We are also keen to reach out to our colleagues in the social services who now have considerable responsibilities for healthcare provision under UK community care legislation. Finally, we are aware that lawyers, police, community support workers, staff in voluntary agencies, education professionals, carers and relatives may all be involved with helping couples who are receiving healthcare and for whom this book may be a source of inspiration. No doubt there will be other groups whom we have not considered, and we apologise for this in advance.

Cultural diversity

Couples from diverse cultures and those who are themselves in alternative lifestyles are often served poorly in health settings in the UK (Nazroo

1999; Palmer and Laungani 1999). This is not just a matter of language or even of institutionalised racism. It is our patients who remind us – if we have the capacity to listen – that Western healthcare sometimes makes assumptions about sexual relationships and sexual behaviour, about being disabled and about the nature of family life. Becoming a patient and adopting a patient role does not always empower patients or service users to take control over their own lives. The cultural and professional prejudices many of us as clinicians carry may aggravate existing power imbalances even further. Meeting couples in health settings affords the clinician a better opportunity to learn about patients and the wider cultural and social context in which they live. We hope that by selecting case examples from as wide a cultural diversity as possible, we will encourage the reader to think more openly and creatively about other people's ways of living, in sickness and in health.

Case examples

Our case examples are fictional, but based in good measure on couples we have worked with or supervised. Our students have requested this and we have chosen examples that not only illustrate our models, but also give the reader a wider picture of applications of a principle or practice. Case studies depict theory in practice, but they can never replicate the experience of the reader who is already working with couples. We present our case examples usually within a counselling format that is understandable to those who have not had psychological or psychotherapeutic training, and we have tried to use straightforward language and avoid technical terms wherever possible.

We hope that when readers have read this book, they will have many more examples clearly in their head that will resonate with the ideas shown here and that will encourage and support them in trying a new way to help the patient more effectively.

Here are some clinical settings and couple dilemmas that could be part of your everyday practice. We hope that this book will help and guide you to appropriate action.

Case study

You are a clinical nurse specialist about to start your busy diabetic outpatient clinic and glance into the waiting room. You are relieved to see Judith, who has had a lot of problems with complying with her treatment and diet, because she has not been attending on a regular basis. She has come with a man whom you have not seen before. When Judith gets up to enter the consulting room, he approaches you and informs you that he is your patient's partner and wants to come into the consulting room with her. You make eye contact with Judith who shrugs and says, rather without conviction, 'He can come in if he wants to'.

What is your response? Should he be invited into the consultation? Is he there to support your patient? Who is the patient? Will he stop Judith talking to you? Will he complain or ask awkward questions?

Conversely, is he there to support the patient? Is he a valuable source of information about why this patient has not been attending or sticking to her regime? Does he help Judith with the daily demands of diabetic healthcare? Does he need to come and tell you his side of the story?

You look to Judith and search for clues. You hope that her face will tell you what to do next and whether this person is to be welcomed, and whether or not he has a role to play in helping your patient to get well and stay well.

Case study

You are an occupational therapist working on a rehabilitation mental health ward. You want to carry out an activities of daily living (ADL) assessment of Bola, a young man with a six-year history of psychosis, four of them spent on the ward. Bola has many problems: he is out of touch with his family of origin, who live in Nigeria, and he has few friends in the UK. You are anxious to complete the assessment because Bola has an opportunity to be resettled in the community if you can help identify his needs. You are interrupted for the second time that morning by an 'urgent' telephone call for Bola from his girlfriend, the mother of his three-year-old daughter, who also has mental health problems. You know that her call will distress your patient and delay the completion of your work, because this has happened before. Bola's girlfriend has already been told by the ward staff that you are on the ward, but she does not make any allowance for that. You begin to feel irritated and want to protect your patient from these intrusions, but at the same time you recognise that his girlfriend is the most important person in his life. Bola makes it clear that he must go to the telephone to talk with her, and leaves the room.

You remain unsure how to proceed. What is the real reason for these calls? Does she want to be included? Does she want to prevent you from working? Should you engage this young woman in what you are doing? Can you help both of them work together to help each other? How and when should you discuss this with Bola's key worker?

Case study

You are a district nurse making a visit to one of your patients in her own home. Ethel is a frail elder who has recently broken her hip, but is recovering well. On this occasion you notice that her husband of nearly sixty years is showing increasing signs of irritation with his wife in your presence and he begins to complain about her unreasonable conduct. He describes endless demands from Ethel for care and attention, which he can longer provide due to his angina. Ethel denies all his allegations and, to your dismay, begins to accuse him of hitting her and bullying her the minute visitors have left the house. They begin to argue in front of you with increasing anger, and both look to you for understanding and sympathy for what is being endured from the other. You look at your watch and realise that you are already late for your next visit.

Are you dealing with a dysfunctional and abusive relationship? Are there risk factors that need to be considered immediately? Should this couple be referred to any specialist services for their problems? Or is this something that can be handled with sympathetic understanding and another visit on your part?

Case study

You are a health advisor running a support group for HIV-positive men in a community clinic. Your patient, Jeremy, has a very low white cell count and you are concerned at his fatigue and increasing difficulty in keeping on top of his illness. Jeremy mentions in the group that his partner of two years has recently threatened to leave him because he finds Jeremy's illness too limiting to his lifestyle. You know that they have practised safe sex since Jeremy first became ill. The group is able to ask Jeremy about his partner's sexual needs, but Jeremy's guilt is very striking, as is his fear of being abandoned. He is also very worried about how or if they will both survive his illness. The group wants to invite Jeremy's partner to join them, but Jeremy makes it clear that he wants nothing of the sort and asks you for your support in the group setting. You try to reassure him, but remain worried about your patient and how to help him with his relationship.

Do you offer to talk to Jeremy alone or encourage him to talk first to his partner? Does the service have any responsibility for the partner, and what are the issues of confidentiality? What is the impact of this failing relationship likely to have on Jeremy's health and ultimate survival?

All these case examples describe how the clinician has an opportunity to seize the moment and make good use of the relationship. How and when to do so is the subject of our text. We do not prescribe correct answers to these dilemmas; rather, we hope that you will at least start to ask yourself the right questions and begin a process with the couple that will help them generate some solutions for themselves.

In our next chapter, we shall consider in more detail some components of couple counselling. These apply universally to all health settings and set the scene for the whole book. There will be more detailed applications of counselling couples in later chapters, where some of these principles will be reintroduced and used in different settings. The purpose of this is to enable readers to see how flexible couple working is and how well it adapts to the needs of patients and their families.

CHAPTER 2

Counselling Skills – engaging the couple

Introduction

The British Association of Counselling (1985), which represents counselling at a national level in Britain, defines 'counselling' as:

> When a person, occupying regularly or temporarily the role of counsellor, offers or agrees explicitly to offer time, attention and respect to another person or persons temporarily in the role of client.

This useful model can be adapted to the health professional's role, inviting a process for changing the feelings, understanding and behaviour of patients. Counselling is non-hierarchical and entails 'coming alongside' the patient. Such a model recognises that the patient and partner have skills that can be used co-operatively in the process. This approach is based more on the *relationship* between the clinician and the couple than on a specific theoretical framework of counselling.

Counselling is not the prerogative of psychotherapists or counsellors. Any clinician successfully engaging with the emotional life of the patient is already using counselling skills. This chapter is designed to help you recognise the skills you use, enhance their use and become more confident with practice. Working with a patient and his or her partner is more challenging, but we believe very worthwhile, and, to some extent, inevitable when you meet the patient and partner together in a healthcare setting.

In a study carried out by One Plus One (Ayles and Reynolds 2001), clinicians who were trying to manage patients with relationship difficulties were asked how they responded. They offered a number of courses of action, the most common of which were to:

- offer support through listening
- offer further sessions or increased visits
- provide advice or information
- consult colleagues for information or advice.

In the study, staff felt they could handle minor problems that were not seen as a direct threat to the relationship. In contrast, they expressed anxiety about more problematic cases. Subjects in the study distinguished minor from major problems according to the couple's own resources, and whatever psychosocial influences and pressures compounded the difficulty. Thus, cultural differences, poverty, poor housing, unemployment and wider family support determined in part how health professionals saw the severity of the problem. Professionals who had received One Plus One's *Brief Encounters* training to work with relationships were more confident about asking direct questions about relationship issues and understanding the limitations of what they could do. The routine use of the Relationship Scale, a tool for screening clients for relationship difficulties (Simons, Reynolds and Morison 2001), was thought to be useful in helping health professionals to identify relationship problems more rapidly and directly.

Ill health is a common source of stress for couples, and stressed couples may become unhealthy. Patients or their partners will frequently use opportunities to seek help for themselves when they have difficulties in their relationships. This can be likened to the 'protest stage' experienced by a child deserted by its mother, which was revealed by the early work on attachment done with the family (Bowlby 1988). It is a healthy response to the personal threat posed by a failing or distressed relationship. A health consultation provides a covert 'ticket of admission' to emotional support, often in the guise of somatic symptoms such as backache, fatigue, poor sleeping patterns or bowel problems. During consultations, the patient or partner has an ideal opportunity to assess and select a sympathetic health professional. Thus, in many situations it is not you who selects a problem you can handle; rather, it is the patient who has chosen *you*. Professionals such as doctors and nurses, who are often perceived as authority figures by the patient, can thus increase the patient's self-esteem and the ability to cope. They achieve this for patients by offering affirmation, an opportunity to clarify the conflicts that are causing distress in their lives and a sense of being valued.

Barriers

Your own anxieties

Throughout this book we have encouraged you as a clinician to invite the couple to share and open up. As a clinician you may feel that the above is a tall order and feel ill equipped to help patients or feel unable to deal with their difficulties in the time available. We understand that you might wonder what can of worms you are opening and be worried about how you will contain the situation. In your anxiety, you may be tempted to ignore clues that the couple are giving you that the relationship is distressed. As we have said, we are not suggesting that you become a couple therapist, although you are already using many of the skills of a therapist. You will see, however, that certain key features are repeated throughout this book and it may be helpful to spend a little time relating them to your personal skills and healthcare setting. We are inviting you to respond empathically, with a clear sense of your boundaries, confident that active listening is a valuable gift to patients. However, some other barriers remain.

Home/work conflict

We know that many health professionals are part-time carers and face the difficulty of balancing home life and a career. Many health workers in their twenties and thirties are raising their children; and an increasing number of health workers in their fifties and sixties are combining work with caring for children, grandchildren and older relatives. This is confirmed by a recent report from The Foundation by the Policy Press (Mooney and Statham 2002). The time constraints of collecting schoolchildren at the end of a clinic or rushing to return to an elderly, infirm parent are a major source of pressure on the clinician trying to work with a distressed patient. Cooper, Sloan and Williams (1988) have shown home/work conflict to be the chief source of occupational stress in nurses.

Organisational conflict

Sutton (1997) reminds us that many practitioners see the introduction of market forces to the practice of health and social care as overturning their central values and vocation as caring professionals. Practitioners are required to spend their time obtaining the best deal for their department, achieving 'throughputs' and 'unit costs', rather than listening to the needs and fears of the distressed patient and family. Organisational conflict stresses the clinician and undermines the motivation to counsel patients or their partners.

Personal baggage

All clinicians carry with them their personal histories and their current perceptions and understanding. When asked, clinicians will provide a whole spectrum of reasons for not being able to listen to patients. They mention the common factors that inhibit all professionals – lack of time, feelings aroused by the encounter with the patient and intuitions or previous experience of the patient. Readers may be facing a personal crisis, a relationship difficulty, a health problem, financial pressures or just the exhaustion and demands of family life and a career (Morrod 2002).

Our personal baggage can also help us to empathise with the problems facing patients; conversely, it can inhibit our response or even cause us to avoid altogether certain patients and their difficulties. For example, a clinician who has recently experienced a spontaneous abortion may find it difficult to work with a woman who is seeking termination of her pregnancy.

It might help to consider the following emotional responses to your clinical work:

- You fear you cannot cope with your own feelings when with certain patients.
- You fear you will not be able to cope with your patients' feelings.
- You are anxious about being overwhelmed by the demands made of you.
- You lack confidence in your skills to listen.
- You believe you have to solve your patients' problems and 'make them better' – part of the ethos of healthcare.

All these processes are capable of undermining our therapeutic effectiveness, but can be addressed through supervision and support and, when necessary, with a personal counsellor.

Brief interventions

Brannen and Collard (1982) have shown that couples are reluctant to admit they have problems in their relationship that they cannot solve themselves, especially in the early stages of the difficulty and very often early in the relationship. This is the very time when an intervention is likely to be most useful to couples and their children. Morrod (2002) recommends a more proactive and less stigmatising approach using health professionals, clergy, social workers and general practitioners. She developed a brief intervention skills model called Brief Encounters for One Plus One to address clinicians' needs. The programme not only trains clinicians in relationship support, but also affirms their role as gatekeepers to relationship support agencies.

Brief Encounters training is designed for busy clinicians who find themselves trying to deal with patients' relationship problems, and has been validated by Corney (1998). The training builds on participants' *existing* skills and gives them the confidence to use listening skills more confidently when contact time with the patient is at a premium. It is intended to help practitioners limit their involvement so that they can approach their patients' problems without fear of being overwhelmed or being unable to extricate themselves when dealing with relationship problems. At the heart of the model are listening skills in clinical settings, but clinicians are also trained in how to recognise the clues or signals from a patient who wants or needs to talk, and how to 'frame an offer' to counsel within the boundaries of clinical practice. In addition, participants can learn how to cope with what the patient and partner discuss, and, finally, how to bring the 'brief encounters' to a mutually satisfactory ending. Training is ongoing and available to UK, Eire and selected overseas readers through One Plus One, Marriage and Partnership Research. Health visitors trained in Brief Encounters screened mothers for relationship problems for the first time in the postnatal period and found some striking results: a quarter of mothers were found to have moderate to severe relationship problems. A follow-up of some of the mothers suggested that almost all received very positive support from their health visitor.

Working with couples

Working with couples involves clinicians in engaging with their relationships. The couple relationship is a complex interaction and, in periods of stability, established patterns of relating will be maintained. This will include power-sharing, responsibility for household chores, decisions about how they spend their recreation time and how they establish intimacy, that is, how emotionally close or how distant they are. An important issue for couples is nurturing: Who is the caring one? Who is the 'sick' one? Who looks after whom? Responsibilities are not necessarily equally divided, e.g. one may appear to hold much of the power in the relationship and make the decisions.

Challenges to this stability come when couples go through a life transition such as pregnancy, retirement or, of course, ill health. The clinician who enters this interaction has an opportunity to witness the patterns between the couple and the ways in which the clinician is drawn into the interactions. Does each partner have a chance to speak? Does one talk for both and the other listen? Does one interrupt the other? Do you empathise with both partners, or collude with one against the other?

The outcome will depend to a large extent on how well the partners communicate and on their ability to organise their relationship so that tasks are accomplished.

Couples who reveal their marital or relationship distress during an illness are likely to be experiencing heightened anxiety, a sense of inadequacy and an inability to deal with the new situation effectively. They may even feel a sense of hopelessness as established ways of dealing with problems have failed and new solutions are needed. Clinicians can help couples to acknowledge how stuck they are and reassure them, as appropriate, that this is a 'normal' response to an abnormal situation. They can enlist the couple's adaptive capacity to reach for new and improved coping patterns. Clinicians have a role to play in assisting communication, checking out understanding and the meanings attached to each partner's words and behaviour. Clinicians can encourage couples to seek achievable solutions. This may require an acceptance of the illness and grieving for the loss of how things might have been.

Counselling skills for engaging the couple

Listening

Counselling skills are often described as relationship-building skills. They help to establish rapport and trust with patients. Health professionals can create opportunities to listen to patients and their families and encourage them to pursue their feelings in a safe and non-judgemental way. At the heart of every good encounter with a patient is the basic and supremely important skill of listening. This applies whether you are giving professional clinical care or trying to help people get the best out of their relationship in the context of healthcare. Sometimes, what is most needed is someone who will *really* listen – not solve problems or come up with answers or solutions, just listen.

A model of social support in pregnancy and around birth devised by Oakley, Rigby and Hickey (1994) was found to be effective in promoting physical and psychological health gain in mothers and babies. *The fact that midwives were prepared to listen was singled out as the most important factor* (our italics).

To listen well, we need to be able to put on hold our own ideas and anxieties, or the panic we experience about where this dialogue is heading. We need a framework for managing time in a brief intervention and clarity about personal and professional boundaries. We have to remind ourselves that we are not responsible for resolving other people's problems, but are responsible for the quality of our listening skills.

Good clinicians already use an extensive range of skills of engagement with their patients. It is useful to enumerate these and increase awareness of them in clinical practice. This approach helps clinicians to value themselves, their competencies and the work they are doing.

Giving information to couples

Patients and their partners in health settings need information about the course of their treatment and care, as well as how they as a couple are responding to the process. Giving information to couples is a three-way conversation. The clinician's task is to provide clear information and check the couple's understanding of it and its impact on them. Many people are helped by visual images or metaphors; here some creativity in imparting information will be appreciated. Leaflets and printed materials that back up the verbal message allow more time for facts to be absorbed and understood. Visual materials should include examples of couples from different cultures and lifestyles. If people are distressed, worried, frightened, distracted, patronised or just not heard, then they will fail to 'hear' the information you are giving them. It is generally helpful to consider how easily you have received information in the past and identify what you found helpful and what was a hindrance. Health professionals have many opportunities to ensure that the couple receive feedback accurately and regularly, and that both can share that information and see areas of agreement or inconsistency about the progress of care.

Clarifying

Clarifying the situation facing the couple is part of the health professional's task. Counselling skills are used to help patients clarify their situation. Clarification can be used to define various problem areas that arise and so form a better idea of the steps that need to be taken. If you simply cannot follow a patient's train of thought or you are not sure what they mean, it is important to ask them to clarify what they are saying. This helps to avoid the risk of misunderstanding or making incorrect assumptions and distorted conclusions. You can use words like 'Are you saying …?' or 'Do you mean …?' or 'I'm not sure I understand what you mean. Would you explain it again, please?'

As in any counselling situation, the patient and spouse may feel unable to face the burden of the health issues that face them and the very particular demands this will make on their relationship. Couples may say 'we're lost' or 'we don't know what's happening' or 'we're frightened to ask'. Individual partners may say, 'I can't tell her what's happening', or 'please don't burden him with that'. These are people who may need time and permission to share their anxieties with a professional who is able to lay out the issues and choices for them. The answer has to be one that allows couples to deal with their distress and generate solutions.

Support in decision-making

Health practitioners are routinely involved in helping patients to make big decisions. At this stage, health workers do not give direct advice; rather, they provide information about options and help clarify issues and discuss health outcomes. It is not possible to support a decision unless the clinician has listened carefully to the couple's understanding of the illness and treatment. A good example of this is the decision whether to receive medical treatments such as kidney dialysis in a hospital or at home. The clinician will provide information about the options available to them. However, the impact on the couple, their family and their home may be considerable. The clinician can support the couple by giving them time to reflect and by providing smaller steps towards the final decision, for example, by introducing them to a renal patient who already has dialysis installed.

Reflecting back

It is important to listen to the words the patient or partner uses and the meaning they attach to them. By reflecting back the content of the words to the couple and the feelings hinted at or expressed, we provide them with a chance to interpret each other's concerns more clearly. The basic skill of reflecting back the content, or paraphrasing the speaker's words, confirms for them that we are struggling to hear and follow their story. Reflecting back builds trust and provides a comfortable pace for the dialogue. It moves the dialogue forward, while creating space for the listener to 'hear' and put a name to the feelings and the message being spoken. When time is short, the most powerful way of moving on is to empathise accurately, particularly when the feelings are strong.

Empathy

Empathy establishes a safe, non-threatening, accepting relationship within which a couple can begin to explore their situation, voice their disquiet and get in touch with needs and feelings. Empathic listening involves *really listening* and working out what the couple are saying, and what the main message is they are trying to convey. It means being non-judgemental and responding with positive regard. In working empathically, we are trying to understand how other people see themselves or their world, from their point of view – rather like standing in the shoes of the patient. This brings us close to being able to name the patients' feelings and experience and give this feedback to patients. It is a skill that requires increased concentration and is often described as active listening. There is a long-established body of evidence (Truax and Carkhuff 1967) which shows that good counsellors offer genuineness, warmth and empathy, whatever their theoretical orientation. Skills matter; but 'congruence' with our patients and a fundamentally positive attitude to them matter more.

Body language

You already have extensive skills in observing the non-verbal behaviour of patients. These skills can be directed towards the patient and partner and enable the practitioner to learn much more about what is happening in the relationship. Body language includes facial expression, gestures, eye contact, tone of voice, physical contact, space between the couple, orientation towards each other and posture. It is often striking how patients' body language changes in the presence of their partners. Health practitioners also communicate through body language: Do we seem too busy, rushed, distracted, anxious or just not interested?

Behavioural changes

Couples may need the professional to create opportunities for behavioural changes in their lives during illness and injury. It is sometimes easier to change behaviour first, and then work out the change in our emotion or thoughts. All behavioural interventions have this as their basic premise. For example, many couples, for a variety of reasons, do not spend time together at meals, or with friends or their children. A small solution they might envisage would be to organise one family meal a day, or the couple spending more time together.

Interpreting

Couples need help in understanding the process of injury or illness, and how this impacts on their sense of themselves as a couple. Health professionals who see both parties have a chance to interpret what is happening to each of them when changes in behaviour or thoughts seem incomprehensible. Professionals understand the role of anxiety, fear, loss, grieving and change on patients, because that is their everyday experience. For the couple, the process may take new and initially incomprehensible forms, all requiring an interpreter.

Cross-cultural skills

All good treatment places the patient in his or her cultural and familial context, because the influence of the context profoundly affects the course of treatment and the way the patient and partner make meaning out of what is happening to them. It is essential that the clinician recognises that healthcare has cultural and gender-specific assumptions and biases. This may be disempowering to all if it is not addressed. For example, women are often the gatekeepers to services for men (Williams 1998).

Supervision and support

Historically, there has always been strict supervision of clinical practice in health management. However, until recently there has been rather less emphasis on personal support and development, and the need for a time and place to stand back and reflect. It is now widely accepted that professional development can be achieved only through continuous learning, supervision and close affiliation to professional bodies. We now recognise the benefits of supervision, based on more traditional psychotherapeutic principles. The purpose of supervision is to maximise the competence of the worker in providing a helping service and to affirm and support the 'helper'. This is achieved by giving space to share thoughts, feelings and pressures and to identify need and celebrate successes. It provides a forum for sharing ideas and information and developing intervention and referral skills. Good supervision allows us to understand the feelings that our patients stir up in us, and how our own baggage is implicated. Supervision gives the clinician support in coping with these feelings and allows us to see patterns and behaviours more clearly – both the patient's and our own. All this enables us to take better care of ourselves and, as a result, better care of our patients and their partners.

Case study

Jenny, a health visitor in her late thirties, recognised that she was edging close to burn-out. She was working in an extremely deprived area and had a heavy caseload. Her father, now elderly and dependent, had been a dominant man, obsessive about financial security. He had earned a reasonable salary, but provided little financial or emotional support for his rather meek wife. Jenny's mother managed by sacrificing her own needs to those of her daughters. She died in her early fifties of breast cancer, which was diagnosed rather late in the process of the disease. She had failed to seek help when she first discovered a breast lump and confided in her nursing daughter only after many months.

The supervisor helped the health visitor to understand her frustrations with patients who fail to fight back, and get better work prospects and a better life for themselves. Jenny began to understand her excessive drive to fight deprivation and injustice. She accepted that she was running a one-woman crusade to put the world to rights and began to prioritise her work, family and relaxation in a new light. She became able to celebrate her own energy and caring, and use both drives more effectively without exhausting herself. Most importantly, she became more able to listen to the parents she worked with and to understand their real concerns and anxieties.

Proctor and Inskipp (1991), both well known for their work and publications on supervision, suggest that:

> If you are to continue in development as a competent and creative worker with people, you need opportunities for:
>
> - Sharing your work in confidence
> - Getting feedback and guidance
> - Developing professional skills, ideas and information
> - Letting off steam if you are angry, fed up or discouraged
> - Acknowledging feelings of distress, pleasure, failure etc.
> - Feeling valued by those you count as colleagues

Referring on

Personal and professional boundaries entail: understanding your task, having 'permission' to work with the patient and partner, knowing your level of competence and curtailing that work if you extend beyond your resources – all of these should help you to know how and when to refer on. We address many of the issues related to referring people on to other professionals in the last chapter of the book.

Guidelines for good practice

The modest aim of counselling in this book is to promote and maintain the health and wellbeing of the patient, by working holistically. It is not about saving partnerships. Even the most skilled couple therapist is limited by what the couple wants to achieve. In health settings, it is appropriate to deal with the illness or injury as it affects both partners, and the extent to which the relationship impacts upon illness.

When you offer a couple or an individual time and attention by listening, you give them a chance to air their feelings and allow them to express their needs and begin to talk about how at least some of those needs can be met. Being with patients in this way helps them face issues more confidently or be strong enough to cope. In addition, patients and partners who are helped to talk and express themselves make their thinking more concrete and clear, and can challenge incorrect ideas or assumptions about each other. Much anxiety and distress in health settings is based on incomplete or false beliefs about the illness and its impact on the patient or partner. Couples who are listened to can express their individual experiences and needs. They can also keep the lines of communication open and are more likely to maintain intimacy in their relationship. Finally, they can find ways of working together and co-operating in a healthcare programme.

When you are with the couple

- Ensure that the couple are seen together.
- Offer the partner initial contact time to compensate for the existing therapeutic contact with patient.
- Allow each to voice his or her concerns.
- Encourage the couple to stay with the 'here and now'. If they raise strong historical themes, such as abuse or past affairs, and cannot deal with the present, consider referring on.
- Demonstrate equal attention and concern to both parties. Look at each in turn. Avoid collusion with one side.
- Look for discrepancies in their stories and in their perceptions, and feed back to the couple.
- Provide factual information to correct any misunderstandings or myths about the illness in the couple's presence.
- When strong emotions are expressed, invite the couple to work out 'what's happening here?'
- Accept a partner's protest about the other as a healthy effort to engage with the relationship.
- Encourage interaction between the couple. Invite them to speak directly to each other whenever possible. Avoid being the main speaker or problem-solver.
- Do not underestimate the opportunity for the couple to use the space and time provided by the clinician to generate solutions.
- Attend to cues. By listening carefully, you may get the feeling that something is not being said or is being tentatively hinted at – maybe just a feeling of underlying distress. Partners or patients may look tired or anxious, or perhaps be neglecting their appearance. If you feel something is wrong, you can create an opportunity for the couple to open up and express their difficulties. It is, of course, important to respect their personal boundaries. Some people are happy to share thoughts and feelings and are grateful for the opportunity. Others find it difficult and may choose not to do so or may take up your offer only when they feel able to trust you more.
- Help people express their experience of conflicting feelings – it can provide considerable relief. Examples include: a patient's desire to talk with a partner conflicting with a fear of denigration; a caring partner wanting acknowledgement, but fearing to burden his wife; a woman wanting to leave an abusive relationship, but feeling bound by duty and guilt to stay with her husband who is wheelchair-bound.

Some important do's

- Relax. Trying too hard makes you feel self-conscious.
- Concentrate on listening. It is easy to be distracted by your own anxieties and what you want to say to reassure.
- Repeat what you have heard to be sure you understand. Unlikely though it seems, this skill of reflecting back does help people to go on talking and stops us interrupting before patients have a chance to say what's really on their mind. For example, if a patient says: 'This last week has been a nightmare. I got 'flu and felt even worse than usual. And the children played up. I just can't cope. I haven't even had time to get my prescription', a good reply would be: 'It sounds as if you had a dreadful week and things got on top of you' rather than, 'Oh yes, half the staff here seem to have had that 'flu as well' as we might be tempted to. This allows and invites the patient to continue and expand on her trials if she wants or needs to.
- Listen carefully for feelings being hinted at or expressed and talk about them, especially strong feelings. Do not be afraid to voice them aloud and help to describe them. For example, a reply to the above patient's statement could just pick up feelings: 'You sound overwhelmed by it all'. If the patient had said 'I can't stand it any more', that is a stronger message and shouldn't be ignored. Acknowledging what you have heard, you might reply: 'You sound as if you are at the end of your tether.'
- Listen carefully for the main message. If you encourage this patient to speak about her problems, does she mainly tell you about how difficult she found it to manage last week or how unsupported and isolated she felt, or is the message really that she is at the end of her tether?
- If the message is really about what a difficult week it was, you might acknowledge how difficult it must have been for her and reassure her that she has done the best she could.
- If, however, she is still exhausted, worried about missing her drug regime and angry with her partner for not being available to help, allow her to express her frustrations and fears. Underneath her frustration or anger with her partner will be hurt and sad feelings. You can address the medical issues, invite her to think about how she might get her partner to help out more or help her think through how she might find other ways of coping. You could offer to see them together and create an opportunity for her partner to share his experiences. He may be unaware of her need, overwhelmed by his own work or trying to cope with a change in his wife's resilience linked to her illness.
- But if you hear a clear message that she is desperate, you will need to encourage her to talk about her feelings, name them for her and consider very seriously whether she needs more help than you can give in

the time available or without more support. Always remember that many people feel considerably better when listened to in this way. Although this may leave you feeling very anxious for them, they feel better for the encounter and more able to deal with their situation.

Some important don'ts

(These notes are adapted from Briefing Notes for encounters with families, One Plus One, 2001.)
There are many responses to patients' distress signals and each will take you by a different path – hopefully, to the same core issues. However, there are a number of unhelpful responses that are best avoided.

- Don't share your personal experience – you may stop the couple communicating. This is their agenda. The patients you are talking to need to believe you are tuning into them directly, not substituting your own experiences.
- Don't judge. Disapproval is the quickest way to stop anyone talking. It is difficult for patients to communicate if they don't feel respected.
- Don't ignore the point. You may want to steer the conversation into more comfortable waters. Perhaps the subject is too close to your own feelings – and your own attitudes can make you feel uneasy. If you decide you are out of your depth, talk to your colleagues or your supervisor. It may be appropriate to refer the couple or the patient on to a helping agency or another professional, (see chapter 10, Endings and Referring the Couple on).
- Don't miss the point – this is related to active listening. If you misunderstand, people are unlikely to keep talking.
- Don't appear distracted – for example, looking round the room, moving away or interrupting.
- Don't advise unless asked – people rarely take unsought advice. You may feel clear about the necessity of giving medical advice, but remember that listening is at the heart of working in partnership with patients. When you are dealing with relationship issues and emotional difficulties it is wise not to advise unless asked. Giving advice comes naturally to most of us, but unless that advice is asked for it is quite often inappropriate and almost certainly ineffective. Wait to be asked, or share ideas and make suggestions very tentatively. For example, you might say, 'Someone I know tried … Do you think that might work for you?' The aim of a good listener is to facilitate patients in working out their own solutions.
- Don't panic. A patient or partner protesting angrily about their partner creates anxiety in helpers, but it may signify that they are still fighting to engage emotionally with their partner.

CHAPTER 3

Sexual Health – the intimate couple

Introduction

This book takes a lifecycle perspective and begins with the couple as sexual beings, who are, at some stage of their lives, in committed sexual relationships. It seems rational, therefore, to give consideration to the sexual health and wellbeing of the couple, and how this might be addressed within the health services. Sexuality will be discussed in other chapters, as there are many opportunities in healthcare to discuss intimacy, but in this chapter we shall focus on how, if at all, it can be addressed in sexual health services. In short, if our patient attends a sexual health clinic, where is the partner, and how might a clinician use the couple's relationship to help both of them in their healthcare?

Historical views

It is paradoxical that the one health setting that specifically deals with human sexuality treats men and women in segregated areas, sometimes using separate entrances and exits, often employing separate staffs, and with little or no acknowledgement of couples, let alone committed relationships.

Historically, there are good reasons for this. Sexual health used to refer to the prevention and containment of sexually transmitted diseases (STDs) – a problem that particularly affected the armed forces at the end of the nineteenth century when these clinics were first established. In the First World War, the British government took what was then the enlightened step of providing anonymous and confidential testing for sexually transmitted diseases, and the tracing of contacts, without name or blame (Bilney and d'Ardenne 2001). Within this model, there were assumptions about the difficulty facing any infected patient in revealing to a partner that the possible source of infection was sexual contact with another person or people.

Whilst this approach has favoured individual patients who are reluctant to reveal the scale and nature of their sexual activity, it does mean that the couple are rarely seen in such a setting in ways that enable them to support and help each other. Clinicians who are trained to give such a high priority to individual confidentiality are also those who can foster open access to, and communication between, the couple. Professional staff in sexual health settings have a unique opportunity to work with couples. They may have to be very opportunistic, and they will certainly be seeing couples in crisis. Staff who are willing to see both partners will be able immediately to help them make choices and changes in their behaviour that will improve their sexual health and level of communication within their relationship.

Clinical settings

Moving out of the trenches

STD clinics have suffered much stigma, being called the 'pox' clinic, the 'special' clinic and, only in very recent years, departments of sexual health. Such a title now embraces a more holistic and less judgemental approach to sexuality, and may cover contraception, fertility, cervical screening, sexual trauma, sexual dysfunctions, psychosexual disorders and HIV/AIDS care. The move to extend the role of sexual health has meant that, for the first time, couples are much more likely to have a legitimate role in this health setting, where both good and bad news may be discussed and shared. Sexual health services may require the involvement of the partner in sharing such news, making decisions, facing crises and ensuring long-term compliance with medical care, often including very challenging drug regimes (Royal College of Nursing 2002). It is very encouraging to see couples coming to sexual health clinics together, clearly committed to seeking care together as partners. It is not always the case that they are treated by the staff with the same degree of enthusiasm or optimism. This reflects in part, we believe, clinicians' lack of confidence and perceived lack of skill in treating couples. Many clinicians also have a cultural reluctance to counsel couples to health maintenance and health gain. We hope that this chapter will address this need in some small measure and will at least encourage the health team to try a different approach.

Barriers within clinical settings

There are many barriers. On the organisational side, there may be few if any facilities that allow the couple to be seen together, either for physical examination or for interview. Heterosexual couples may still face physical separation, separate staff and case notes that are identified by a number only, and all segregated by gender. Most staff working in sexual health are trained to interview and examine the individual, and make reference to the partner or partners with the identified patient. If a partner arrives at the clinic, practitioners have been known to perceive the partner at best as a nuisance, and at worst as compromising confidentiality and accurate history-taking.

This is understandable. Many sexual health patients who arrive alone do not tell the truth about their marital or relationship status, and there is some evidence to show that men give more false information than women (Bilney and d'Ardenne 2001). The reasons why remain unclear, and the current culture in sexual health is unlikely to provide access to patients' motives in distorting or omitting information. Patients who see a doctor of their own sex are more likely to be truthful, and there is anecdotal evidence that patients provide different types of information to medical and non-medical staff in sexual health settings. It would seem that patients want to present themselves more favourably to doctors than other sexual health clinicians, and that this is independent of the skill of the practitioner involved. There are implications here that the person who obtains a fuller sexual history may not be the examining physician.

The most common falsehood is that patients say they are unattached when they are in a committed relationship. Whilst this is very understandable, the implications are potentially disastrous. Sexual health staff are often aware of this, but can do little to educate the patient about preventing further infection. Misinformation from patients leaves a pool of infected, untreated and uninformed individuals. A changing culture where patients see other couples regularly attending sexual health clinics would, we believe, go some way in persuading the infected party that there is no shame in acting responsibly and bringing his or her regular partner for a check-up.

In the UK there is a good method of accessing the untreated partner via the health advisor, who has an important role in partner notification (previously known as 'contact tracing'). This system is now universally used and has a significant impact on breaking the chain of disease transmission and reducing overall rates of STD infection (SHASTD 1993). Oxman et al. (1993), however, have noted that partner notification may have negative effects on the patient's social wellbeing. Trust in the relationship may be compromised; it may even precipitate violence. Understandably, patients who are married or in a committed partnership experience fear, shame and/or anxiety about their sexual health if they have had multiple partners.

The picture is more complex when a patient who has had only one sexual partner is diagnosed with a sexually transmitted disease. In clinic, this 'innocent' partner may greet the diagnosis with shock and denial, followed by anger and eventually depression as the realisation about their partner's unfaithfulness sinks in. The clinician has to encourage the patient to speak with the partner and work with both of them if at all possible, and as quickly as possible. Again, a change of culture in the working practice of health professionals to become more couple-focused will assist in this transition.

Same-sex partnerships in clinical settings

Same-sex partners face similar challenges to those of heterosexual partners in health gain; the issues around sexual health are no exception. The research literature on sexual health has focused on sexually transmitted disease and much less on the specific issues within the relationship. The proliferation of government funding for HIV/AIDS prevention and treatment in the last two decades has at least ensured that the disease aspect of being gay has received attention, but much less attention has been given to how committed relationships may make health gains and treatment decisions easier to sustain.

Butler and Clarke (1991) and Simons (1991) have looked at some of the issues facing same-sex partnerships and have summarised the issues for clinicians. These include:

- the need for clinicians to deal with their own homophobia, which can often be masked behind avoidance or an overemphasis on medical treatment
- helping the gay couple themselves deal with their own homophobia/lack of self-esteem, especially in relation to their family of origin
- asking about and responding to individual and couple difficulties in coming out and
- dealing with changes in sexual practice that result from a diagnosis, and helping the couple own the decision for that change.

The sexual and relationship needs of gay couples in the past were a neglected topic and need to be addressed by health staff (d'Ardenne 1999). Significantly, the sexual orientation of the counsellor is not likely to influence the outcome in working with gay or lesbian couples; what is, is the openness of that counsellor to recognising and considering alternative lifestyles. Failure to do this will result in many same-sex couples not using statutory sexual health services – or at least withholding information about their partnership if they believe that the clinician does not want to hear about it. There is a little evidence (Bilney and d'Ardenne 2001) to suggest that this is more true for lesbian couples than gay men, but the effect is nevertheless worrying. Greene (1994) has expressed this more forcefully: 'therapists must begin to assess the impact of a legacy of negative stereotypes about gay men and lesbians on their own thinking and they must do so before a gay or lesbian ever appears before them.'

Transcultural settings for couples

It can be argued that all couples find themselves in cross-cultural settings; but in sexual health, clinicians will often be working with couples who come from a different ethnic, national and/or socio-economic background from their own. Couples will differ from the clinician and also from each other, and there are important issues for the practitioner to understand before being able to offer counselling that has value to the patient and partner (d'Ardenne et al. 1990; d'Ardenne and Mahtani 1999). One of these is that the whole concept of counselling people as a way of dealing with personal difficulty is itself an expression of Western individualistic culture, which traces its practice origins to Freudian and Rogerian theory. Counselling couples from a different cultural background requires at least an awareness that patients and partners may be looking for education, advice or cure, but not necessarily counselling. There are other reasons. Dominelli (1988) argues that the dominant culture has an expectation that assimilation will result in couples from other cultures absorbing many of its values and perceptions, and that this will in some way mitigate many of the problems connected with the daily experience of racism. Such a position relieves health services of any responsibility to create a more diverse, positive or welcoming clinical setting.

Some clinical services make assumptions about couples from diverse cultures that lead to their being sent to 'specialist' community services, because clinicians believe that mainstream health services do not or cannot offer counselling and support that is culturally sensitive. Here again, clinicians retain a sense of powerlessness about working with patients and their partners whom they see as having needs that they cannot address. While minority ethnic community services may be culturally appropriate, they are not always very skilled in healthcare practice. What is more, couples do not necessarily want to be seen outside mainstream services; they may already feel marginalised and are entitled to healthcare with a professional interpreter if that is required. It is the responsibility of the service to ensure that patients and partners who do not speak English are seen with an interpreter, and that the partners are not required to interpret for each other, unless that is their choice.

Clinicians already have cross-cultural skills, but are often unaware of them. The attitudes, expectations, experience, knowledge, education and generic investigative skills of the clinician will help staff working in departments of sexual health to create a positive, respectful and effective clinical setting (d'Ardenne 1988; Hooper and Dryden 1991).

Examples of differences between Western and non-Western cultural thinking about counselling couples include:

- the relative significance of past or future events – Western history-taking versus a non-Western focus on the present
- the importance of traditional family values
- individualism versus the role and obligations of the individual to the community
- Western scientific versus non-Western intuitive thinking.

The different roles of the sexes in other cultures

Think about your existing cross-cultural resources and competencies. As well as having access to libraries and institutions that can give you information about other cultures, you may have family experience of living with another culture; social networks, neighbours and friends from other cultures; spiritual or religious experiences that promote tolerance and understanding of other cultures; other cultural healthcare experience, e.g. Yoga, T'ai Chi; education and training across cultures; political community activities; travel; and employment policies that promote positive, multicultural working.

D'Ardenne and Mahtani (1999) asked clinicians working with patients from outside their own culture the following questions:

- Can you accept, acknowledge and understand your couple's culture?
- Do your expectations about the clients' culture affect the counselling outcome?
- Does your cultural prejudice have any bearing on the counselling relationship?
- Does any cultural prejudice or racism experienced by you have any bearing on the counselling process?
- Are your expectations of outcome within a Western model likely to affect the counselling relationship and outcome?

Types of couple problems

Sexual dysfunction

In recent years the concept of sexual wellbeing has just begun to replace the palliative model in sexual health clinics. Couples are now more likely to be invited to discuss their mutual sexual needs and interaction. Some services provide trained sexual therapists who assess and treat couples with a range of problems of libido and sexual functioning. As in so many health settings, the gateway to care may start with the couple seeking treatment for physical symptoms, then open up to psychological issues, before finally revealing the sexual relationship and any difficulties linked to it.

Case study

John refers himself to the sexual dysfunction clinic because of post-coital pain. During the history-taking, it becomes clear that he ejaculates before he is able to penetrate his current partner, Ellen. He has suffered with this for some years with several partners, but it has now become much worse. A diagnosis of premature ejaculation is made. The nurse sees a window of opportunity to invite John and Ellen in to take a fuller sexual history to establish whether there is the possibility of involving Ellen to help John to gain ejaculatory control.

John agrees to invite Ellen in to share the problem with her and the nurse by describing in detail what happens when they attempt intercourse. They also disclose to the nurse their shared anxiety that the relationship will not survive because of the sexual problem. Ellen believes that she is the cause of John's pain and premature ejaculation. The nurse listens to this couple's sadness and responds by asking them if they would favour a practical and shared approach to 'their' difficulty. She explains the basic principles of behavioural intervention. This involves the couple in sharing responsibility for the problem and communicating and working together at home, as well as sharing their progress in clinic with the nurse.

John and Ellen are asked initially to agree mutually and voluntarily to abstain from sexual intercourse or attempts at intercourse. This immediately removes from John the fear of failing during sexual performance, and from Ellen the experience of being a failed lover. It also allows them the space to learn a new way of having sex. They then agree to set aside time at home to learn a series of graded exercises to increase sensual pleasure and communication. During this intervention, John and Ellen learn how to recognise and then control John's ejaculatory response and then his pre-ejaculatory response. The couple are next trained in gradual sexual activities that approximate more and more to intercourse until they both feel more in control. The breakthrough in their sexual functioning frees both of them to address other anxieties with more confidence and more optimism.

Such an intervention is possible only when both partners are fully informed and involved with the treatment programme. It is a good example of how healthcare might be better directed at the couple once the practitioner has had a chance to meet them and engage in their distress.

Fertility

Couples may be asked to attend departments of sexual health when information and decisions have to be made about fertility. Many sexually transmitted diseases reduce fertility and both parties need to be briefed about the findings and their plans. They may go through a period of mourning for the children they will never have. There may also be further decisions to make about the viability of the relationship, if one party is presumed to be fertile, but the other is not. The role of the clinician at this stage is to ensure that such a process at the very least does not compromise the wellbeing of the patient, and that every help can be afforded to the couple, who may now have to make choices that extend well beyond their immediate health concerns.

Case study

Jean has been investigated for infertility and has been given a diagnosis of chlamydia. She is married and has been trying to start a family with her husband, Paul. She has been told by the physician that as a result of the infection, which she did not know she had, she and Paul have a very poor chance of conception. Jean is devastated by the news and is worried about its effect on her marriage. They have always wanted children and she fears that Paul will be resentful and blaming at discovering he has no choice. Jean also needs advice on her current health and the need to have more regular check-ups.

The health advisor invites Jean and Paul to the clinic to provide them both with as much information as possible about Jean's diagnosis. The clinician shares the implications for fertility with them in a non-judgemental way. By being more objective, the health advisor hopes to provide a safe place to explore their feelings and the impact of this news on their relationship. Both are asked by the advisor to repeat what they have understood from the doctor about Jean's fertility and are given a chance to correct any misunderstandings they may have about Jean's health. They are then encouraged to talk through their sense of loss and are given permission to express their sadness and grief. At the end of the session the advisor arranges to see them again. She will then check whether, if at all, they have had a chance to talk to each other and make any more sense of what has happened to them. The clinician will refer them for specialist counselling if she thinks that the couple are no longer able to contain this event and integrate it into their life.

HIV/AIDS care

The diagnosis of HIV can precipitate a crisis forcing an examination of the patient's lifestyle and sexual practices. Gay men, for example, will face uncertainties about this and about disclosure to their families of origin as well as their partners. Bisexual men may face other problems. Their heterosexual relationship may be interwoven with casual gay sex. Heterosexual patients are often reluctant to see themselves as even having been at risk, and may remain bewildered and angry. The HIV diagnosis leaves patients in a state of great fear and often wanting to blame others. It may, for example, lead to confronting the partner with his or her lifestyle and range of sexuality and behaviour. More emotional crises will ensue, precipitating either a break-up or a consolidation of the partnership. Either way, the patient who is in a relationship will be entering a new phase of decision-making, and one with which the health advocate is in a unique position to help. If the couple are to continue sexual relations, they may have to do so using barrier methods of contraception. There may be reluctance to do this, especially if this does not correspond with their cultural beliefs about vulnerability to disease.

A good example of this is the (erroneous) idea that women can infect men with the HIV virus, but that men cannot infect women.

In such a situation, the health worker may have to shift the focus from trying initially to correct such beliefs to encouraging health compliance by whatever means possible.

Case study

Marie is of Rwandan origin and has recently been given a diagnosis of HIV. She has not shared the diagnosis with her partner, Bernard, nor the fact that she has unprotected sex with other partners. She fears his violence if he learns the truth, and even more than this, fears that he will abandon her and that she will die alone. She does not believe that Bernard is at risk. The health advisor asks her to explain this, and she describes how, in her culture, many men believe that only 'weak' men succumb to the virus. Bernard thinks in this way.

By careful question and answer, the health advisor is able to persuade Marie that it might be safer to have protected sex with all her partners to protect her own health. She agrees with Marie about how much information can be disclosed and invites Marie and Bernard to attend the clinic together. She advises Bernard that Marie is very ill and that barrier methods will need to be used to keep her well. No more information is given than is absolutely necessary to ensure he complies with safe sex. He asks about the diagnosis in a vague way. The health worker advises Bernard that it is important for Marie to avoid pregnancy (true), but does not volunteer why. Bernard appears more concerned about whether he will be able to have sex at all with Marie. Marie is able to reassure him and both agree to attend a second session to establish compliance with her medication and with protected sex.

It is planned that, as and when Bernard returns and begins to express more interest in Marie's illness, he will be ready to hear more of the truth in a controlled setting. The health advisor discusses this case with the team, and a senior colleague agrees to be available at short notice to break the bad news. The team also makes suggestions to the advisor about culturally appropriate information in French, how to prevent further infection, as well as how to anticipate Marie's fears concerning her situation.

Sexual violence

Rape victims are often seen in STD clinics for routine testing and may or may not be accompanied by their partners. Rape is primarily an act of violence, but its sexual nature may leave the partner feeling angry about not being there, and/or ashamed about not having been able to prevent the crime. By the same token, the victim may feel angry with the partner who was not there when the attack took place and who may be blamed for 'allowing it to happen'; on the other hand, he may be the object of fear and loathing because he is the same sex as the assailant. The victim may receive support and counselling; but the partner is often neglected and may feature only if he or she is at risk of a sexually transmitted disease, or if there is a court case pending.

Many rape cases are not reported to the police (Kershaw et al. 2000), but are known to the health services. These can pose legal as well as clinical issues for the health professional working with patient and partner.

Case study

Annie attended a sexual health clinic because she initially reported to her GP that she no longer had any interest in sex and was non-orgasmic. During routine assessment, it became clear to the nurse that Annie was regularly having sex with customers in her husband's shop under duress. Her husband, Ron, owed a great deal of money to various creditors, and Annie, having been threatened and put under pressure, had agreed to have sex with them. She feared that if she did not, Ron would become the victim of robbery, extortion or personal violence. She did not see that she herself had become a victim of such violence and that crimes were being committed against her. She refused point blank to go to the police about her situation and was very unhappy about sharing any of her distress with Ron, whom she felt already had too much to cope with.

The nurse was able to persuade Annie that her loss of sexual desire was directly related to the stress of non-consensual sex. Furthermore, Annie was persuaded to bring Ron into the clinic for a 'routine' check on his sexual health, and for them to talk about what they both wanted from their relationship. They began to address ways of increasing intimacy and keeping Annie well. After Annie had brought Ron to the clinic, she was able to return to the nurse later and talk about ways of keeping herself safer. She had been touched by the nurse's concern for her wellbeing and for her marriage, and she was able to make a decision to find other ways of responding to and sharing her husband's financial difficulties.

Paraphilias (sexual minorities/sexual deviance)

Couples can present with a problem when one of them develops a sexual attachment to something outside the relationship. Examples include cross-dressing, sadomasochism, trans-sexuality, sexual exhibitionism, voyeurism or any kind of fetish. It is worth remembering that paedophilia and incest also come within this category. Sometimes it will be the partner who mentions the problem; occasionally the person with the sexual preference will ask for help. The tensions that can be created in the partnership (and in the clinician) can be enormous, especially if children are involved. Some paraphilias are within the law, some clearly are not; it is worth remembering though that only twenty years ago homosexuality was regarded as a sexual deviation requiring treatment from psychiatric services. Nevertheless, the spouse who discovers her husband is gay may derive little comfort in the change in the law. Meanwhile, there are few pornographic magazines on display that do not appeal overtly to one kind of sexual minority or another.

Our legal sanctions are determined by social attitudes and our personal response is shaped by our knowledge, culture and sexual attitudes. It is often the case that a couple will approach a clinician in the hope that a 'cure' will be found for the partner's 'illness'. However, the partner with the sexual preference may be seeking tolerance for behaviour that is clearly distressing to or alienating the other, and may seek collusion with the clinician against an intolerant spouse. As with so many issues in human sexuality, the clinician needs to ask: What is the trigger? Why are the couple disclosing these issues now? What are they willing to consider in terms of change? The clinician should discuss these in supervision and become fully acquainted at least with the child protection policies of the team/employer. She will also consider referral to specialist mental health services, if appropriate.

Guidelines for good practice

Couples who are given shared information at the start of healthcare have a chance to make sense of what is happening in their relationship and the changes that may be required, often quite urgently. The health professional may assume that the couple is preoccupied with disease transmission and coping with the illness and treatment, whereas the challenges the couple face may be more wide-ranging (Smith 1997). They also need to continue to make everyday decisions about finances, their employment, having and bringing up children and moving house. Couples can become preoccupied with a diagnosis or, conversely, avoid discussion for fear of raising further anxiety in the partner. Many professionals feel anxious about couple issues. Seeing both partners takes more time, is more complex and makes more emotional demands of the clinician. Once these realities have been accepted, however, the clinician can progress towards better communication, shared goals, better support for the patient, increased treatment compliance (Royal College of Nursing 2002) and, ultimately, prevention and improved outcomes.

Being non-judgemental

It is essential that the health professional remains non-judgemental, whilst acknowledging the distress of the infected partner. We saw in an earlier case study that Jean was shocked and ashamed of her previously acquired infection and its impact on her marriage. The clinician's impartiality provided her with the space to consider her predicament in a more rational way and gave her permission to discuss her diagnosis with her partner with as many of the facts as possible. This does not mean that clinicians do not have moral positions on sexual behaviour; rather, that when they are with their patient, they are mindful of where they stand and use the time in counselling to allow the patient to make his or her own moral choices.

Being comfortable in one's own sexuality

An important principle of good practice in working in the domain of sexual wellbeing is that as clinicians we understand a little of our own sexual attitudes, behaviour, preferences, ignorance and prejudices. Whether or not we are sexually active, our sexuality is a both personal and universal characteristic, which permeates everything we do and say about ourselves.

Not only this, but our sexuality changes with our life experience. For example, the clinician who has had children will have a different perception of sexual standards from those she held when she was sexually inexperienced. Supervision in the health team is a model for best practice for learning to recognise our sexual attitudes, dealing with the parts of us that are not at ease with ourselves, and which are ultimately reflected in our discomfort with the sexual behaviour of our patients.

Working with the team

Sexual health care is typically provided on a multidisciplinary basis. There is some evidence to show that the best referrals are made through regular discussion, supervision or peer discussion (d'Ardenne et al. 1990). Good practice requires excellent written communication and advice from other team members, who may well be in contact with the partner. It is also easier to deal with problems early if it appears that referral to more specialised psychotherapy or mental health services is likely to be needed.

Confidentiality

Confidentiality in sexual health is of paramount importance. Health practitioners have always spent time in clinic explaining to individual patients the value of confidentiality and the practical steps the clinic takes to ensure that names and identities are not divulged. This may have been true historically when partners were perceived as 'contacts' in the transmission of disease. Good practice with the couple still requires the same attitude towards confidentiality, but with the added dimension of encouraging open communication between the couple. A partner who is present in the clinic is evidence that the couple are already tackling some sexual health issues on a shared basis. They need that to be acknowledged and appreciated. The practitioner is able to describe the difference between secrecy and confidentiality, and reassure the couple that confidentiality is not compromised from the clinic's standpoint.

Communication

Working with two people is hard work; there is more than twice as much happening as when there is only one patient. Try to allow more time for each partner to talk and keep checking that each has heard correctly what has already been shared, by asking questions. Place both members of the couple at an angle to you so that all three parties can maintain eye contact throughout the interview.

Identifying myths

As an extension of communication, much of the message of the sexual health professional is spent identifying false information or 'myths' about human sexuality and inviting the couple to generate alternative explanations about what they already understand. Zilbergeld (1980) describes a range of false beliefs (myths) about sexuality that pervade the thinking of individuals in intimate partnerships. These include such ideas as:

- Men should always initiate sex.
- You can tell if a man is aroused by the strength of his erection.
- Women are the partners who are meant to show emotion.

More relevant (and perhaps more dangerous) myths about sexual health include:

- 'Real' men do not contract HIV.
- Only men can pass the virus to other men and women.

An important feature of good practice in counselling in sexual health is that the couple are not confronted with the falsehood of their beliefs, nor indeed confronted with anything else. Rather, they are invited to see if there is any evidence to support them or if the evidence is inconsistent or unverifiable. They are then asked to generate an alternative explanation of their world that makes better sense of their experience and to begin trying to see if it is true.

Lastly, a checklist for couple work

- Is the patient in any type of committed sexual relationship?
- Have I made assumptions about my patient's sexual orientation?
- Have I made cultural assumptions about my patient or about my patient's partner?
- Do my assumptions create a barrier to my clients?
- How do my sexual prejudices influence my work in sexual health?
- Does the patient communicate need for work with his or her partner?
- Why are they seeking help now?
- Are they likely to have a shared agenda for working?
- Are they motivated to work together with or without professional input?
- Where are the couple in their thinking and understanding, now that they have been seen together in the sexual health clinic?
- Do they need referral to another agency?
- Are there any legal implications to discuss with my supervisor?
- Will I be offering them further time?

CHAPTER 4

Antenatal Care – the expectant couple

Introduction

Couples have not always been welcome in antenatal care. Lorna Sage (2001) describes in her autobiography her experience of arriving for her confinement, being hustled into the delivery room and her husband promptly bundled back into the ambulance to be taken home. 'So mothers were dirt and fathers hardly came into it at all, for visiting hours were brief and the hospital was nearly impossible to reach by bus. There were no public phones. The ward was the world.' The year was 1960. Thirty-six years later a Health Education Authority publication stated: 'The birth of a baby brings in its wake major disruption in all areas of life, which is readily acknowledged by parents. They report suffering significant emotional upheaval and disruption of existing intimate relationships – especially with their partners' (Rogers et al., 1996).

The working model used by antenatal support workers would seem to be important in providing appropriate emotional and social support for families with young children. In fact, the psychological impact and relationship issues surrounding birth and becoming parents are now well recognised by health professionals: emotional support to parents is clearly as important as the advice given.

This chapter focuses on the impact of pregnancy, birth and early parenting on the couple and their relationship in healthcare settings. Other chapters cover sick children, sexual health, postnatal mental health problems and violence in the partnership; these topics also feature briefly in this chapter.

History

It is possible to pick up an obstetric handbook published only thirty years ago and find not a single reference to fathers, parents, partners or sex

(Sweet and Cape 1976). In fact, it is only relatively recently that a serious effort was initiated within our culture to involve the couple in the birth (Leboyer 1977; Kitzinger 1980). This drew plenty of opposition from both traditionalists, who saw the man as a nuisance or, at best, someone to be tolerated in the delivery room, and those of a more feminist disposition. The latter saw the man as an oppressor and unwelcome in a domain where women were finding their new selves – presumably with female friends and relatives.

The role of fathers and mothers within our culture is now commonly featured and dissected in the media and creates a vast field for discussion and dissent, ranging from 'working mothers' to increased surgical intervention in the birth process. Foetal monitoring, scans and other procedures give couples access to a vast range of information about the pregnancy. However, increased surveillance also raises uncertainties and generates new dilemmas and decisions for the parents. Live births per thousand may have improved, but there has been a price to pay. It is not hard to imagine couples struggling to make sense of additional information and research findings about diet, lifestyle, exercise, antenatal education, medical indicators and risk factors. The information may be contradictory and incomplete, with little time to question and understand the implications.

The emotional impact and anxieties raised by health surveillance, which are currently being discussed in the media and among medical professionals, were widely commented on by parents in a study commissioned by the Health Education Authority (Rogers et al. 1996). 'The "care and support" element, which was a starting point for professional principles and practice of ante-natal care, has gradually been transformed over a thirty-year period to a point where it has taken on the character of a technological surveillance programme' (Oakley 1988).

Rationale

The couple relationship is pivotal to individual and family wellbeing. Conflict and marital breakdown are associated with the development of emotional and behavioural difficulties in children (Reynolds 2001) and an increased risk of poor mental and physical health for spouses (McAllister 1995). The couple relationship is particularly vulnerable to difficulties during the perinatal period. A range of studies shows that partners experience a drop in marital satisfaction and an increase in conflict over the transition to parenthood (Cowan and Cowan 1992; Sanders, Nicholson and Floyd 1997). Research has also identified an association between relationship difficulties and postnatal depression (O'Hara and Swain 1996) and an increase in domestic violence during the perinatal period (Mezey and Bewley 1997). Books abound on the physical changes that occur during pregnancy, information about birth and guidance on raising children. However, it is rare to find more than a paragraph – or at most a page – on the impact on parents as a *couple* and the support they need. This omission persists despite research studies confirming that the quality of the parental relationship is central to children's wellbeing (Reynolds 2001).

Many clinicians are daunted by the prospect of helping couples talk about their relationship (Ayles and Reynolds 2001). Yet research studies suggest that individuals experiencing relationship problems turn to health professionals at this time, and with appropriate training and resources, members of the primary care team are well placed to offer support and information (Simons, Reynolds and Morison 2001).

The role of emotional support

A model of social support in pregnancy and around birth devised by Oakley, Rigby and Hickey (1994) was found to be effective in promoting physical and psychological health gain in mothers and babies. Midwives' willingness to listen was singled out by parents as the most important factor. Antenatal support workers are in a prime position to offer emotional support to parents when they experience pregnancy and the birth of a child. During this time of change, when contact with health professionals is at a peak, intervention may be most effective. Even a brief intervention can help, if patients and their partners are listened to and allowed to reveal their underlying emotions and emerging difficulties.

However, midwives and health visitors are under enormous pressure to cope with a busy workload, falling numbers of colleagues and changes to their role within primary healthcare. Many health professionals themselves experience the frustration of not being listened to or heard within their working environment. They can, therefore, understand patients' need for someone to listen to them and take them seriously – particularly during change or transition. With current policy drivers such as NHS plans, the development of Primary Care Trusts and 'Sure Start', the role of the midwife appears set to expand. New policies encourage a more flexible and holistic role for midwives. They will need to take a broader approach to health and family wellbeing and may provide postnatal care up to and including the infant's six-week check. In these wider roles, midwives will be in a strong position to work more closely with couples during their transition to parenthood.

Transitions – from partners to parents

A transition may be described as the process of changing from one state of life to another, such as a young girl starting menstruation or young people leaving home. From the cradle to the grave, we all move through many biological, psychological or social transitions.

Couples experiencing the major transition of becoming parents inevitably face developmental changes, and their response to each other and the new child is shaped by their shared resources and capacity for change. If they are unable to cope with the internal or external stresses of transition, both negative and positive, they will seek help from those around them. They will most likely turn to family and friends, or the health professionals they meet routinely in healthcare settings. Clinicians who are aware and skilful at listening and picking up cues have an opportunity to offer timely and effective help. Typically, women in a state of crisis find it easier to seek help than men. Yet crisis presents an opportunity for the couple to regain their equilibrium and even enhance their partnership. A minimum of therapeutic intervention during the brief crisis period can often produce a maximum therapeutic effect. Practice-derived wisdom suggests that access to help should be available early and that help is best timed at the onset of a crisis. The goal of crisis intervention is to reduce stress and sustain the client's coping (Parad and Parad 1990).

Periods of transition are also times of risk. Balakrishna (1998) has shown that 'domestic' violence typically erupts most often during the first pregnancy. Midwives and antenatal support staff have an opportunity to work with families at an early stage to reduce the risks of postnatal depression, domestic violence and couple conflict. These are all factors that are associated with relationship difficulties and have been shown to have a long-term, deleterious impact on both the infant and the parents. The health professional has unique access to the couple at this transition and needs heightened awareness of early signs.

Women who have been violently attacked are more than twice as likely as other women to have a miscarriage or stillbirth (Andrews and Brown 1988). Miscarriages, pre-term labour and bleeding during pregnancy are associated with physical violence. Increased alcohol consumption, verbal aggression, withdrawal, cancelled antenatal appointments and classes, and sleep and appetite disturbance in the mother may all indicate stress within the relationship.

Clinical settings

Pregnant women and their partners rapidly come into the health domain. The GP, family planning nurse or midwife needs to be aware of the impact on the parents-to-be, from the first contact confirming the pregnancy, to delivery and family life. A pregnancy represents a developing and fundamental shift in any relationship. At any stage of the pregnancy, therefore, the mother's relationship with herself and her partner demands the attention of the health professional.

Most antenatal services are initiated in primary care during the initial testing for pregnancy, although pregnancy tests can now be carried out at home. However, it will be the mother's family doctor (GP) who will commence care and refer her to antenatal services throughout her pregnancy. The health professionals most likely to be involved with early pregnancy may well find themselves dealing with relationship issues. At this stage, the woman is the identified patient as antenatal classes may be the father's first contact with the healthcare system and his main source of information and support about the pregnancy.

For many couples, the GP and midwife will remain the key clinicians in the management of pregnancy, but complications may precipitate the mother into secondary specialist medical care. Examples of this include obstetrics, diabetics, coronary care, haematology, renal units and oncology. Some women will develop puerperal psychosis and will be admitted with their newborn into a mother and baby unit for monitoring and psychiatric care. In fact, a pregnant patient can end up in almost any medical or community health setting.

There remains a small number of women who must be seen in a clinical setting without their male partners. Mother and baby units, which offer beds to new mothers with mental disorders, may need to ensure a safe place away from their partners and other men. This clinical setting will also include women with or without a baby, who are the victims of domestic violence.

Violence between the couple

Pregnant women and women with children are more likely to experience domestic violence than women without children. Thirty-five per cent of women surveyed reported experiencing an increase of violence during pregnancy (Hillard 1985) and repeated episodes of violence are common during pregnancy (McFarlane et al. 1992). Care settings are often not appropriately structured to allow the privacy and time needed to explore the woman's problems and maternity care has more recently, explicitly tried to involve partners in all aspects of care. The Department of Health's report (1994–96) on confidential enquiries into maternal deaths in the UK, restates the Royal College of Obstetricians and Gynaecologists' (RCOG) recommendation that all women be seen on their own at least once during their antenatal care. It also recommends the routine inclusion of enquiries about domestic violence when taking a social history for all pregnant women and the provision of an interpreter if necessary (Home Office 2000).

Healthcare professionals are often isolated from other agencies with an active role in offering victims support. They need education, clear protocols and good links for referral.

Couple problems

However close couples feel before the baby is born, they may find that their worlds seem to be moving in opposite directions after the birth. There never seems to be any time to talk to each other. Difficulties arise, do not get sorted out and can grow into barriers to spoil the closeness previously enjoyed. For some couples the agenda may be complex – for example, a woman's partner may not be the father of the child.

> The stresses imposed by parenthood can provoke or intensify relationship problems between parents. These problems, which are often associated with post-natal depression, can have serious consequences for family well-being but are often not revealed to primary health care personnel. (Simons, Reynolds and Morison 2001)

Simons, Reynolds and Morison's important study looked at 1,000 live births. The authors found that women attending intervention clinics with trained health visitors using a relationship screening tool were four times more likely than controls to reveal relationship problems at the 6–8 week check, and six times more likely to be offered help. What is more, the subjects usually welcomed such help.

The age at which a pregnancy occurs can be a problem for the couple. Rates of teenage pregnancy in the UK are among the highest in Europe. The partner, or father of the baby, may be absent. Very young couples are struggling with their own growing up and separation from their families of origin. Many teenage mothers fail to complete their full-time education, and the subsequent economic and social outcomes for the couple may be long-term poverty and social exclusion. All statistics confirm the enormous difficulties that teenage couples have in maintaining commitment to each other during the stress of a pregnancy – planned or otherwise (Simons 1999). Midwives are aware that some pregnant teenagers have a poor attendance record at antenatal clinics and that these mothers incur subsequent risks during their pregnancy. Some girls feel uncomfortable with the system; some do not attend at all because they want to hide the pregnancy from others. As a consequence, projects exist in which midwives and health professionals target teenage parents.

At the other end of the reproductive life-cycle, women in their thirties and beyond are planning their first babies. Couples have to face the decline in their own fertility with age, and the strain that waiting and then fertility testing and counselling place on the couple's relationship. More women than ever are now employed, and the home/work balance remains a challenge for both partners.

Sex during pregnancy

This is a topic that often causes anxiety for antenatal staff. A simple question may often be followed by a whole range of anxieties expressed by the couple about the effect of intercourse on the pregnancy: Will it damage the baby? Couples may also fear miscarriage if the woman is orgasmic, since they associate uterine contractions with labour. It is helpful to ask couples which, if any, of these they fear, and what it is they do in their current lovemaking that tries to avoid such problems. Couples often appear to be asking for information, when they are actually seeking reassurance.

Birth and coping afterwards

The birth of a child and subsequent care of the newborn infant require a major adjustment by a couple and can test their resources considerably. Birth is a time of disruption caused by the demands of the baby, which at times may seem overwhelming. Added to the exceptional demands, particularly on the mother, are profound physical and emotional changes. A baby tends to stir up all sorts of unconscious issues and can 'give birth' to unexpected problems. Much of what we have learned about parenting comes from our family of origin and lies buried so deep within us that we are unaware of it. If these are bad or distressing memories, they can be triggered unexpectedly by the birth, affect behaviour and puzzle the partner.

Some women find it difficult to adapt to the changes in their bodies throughout pregnancy and after childbirth, particularly if a partner is critical or lacks understanding. They may feel unattractive or concerned not only about gaining weight and external changes in their bodies, but also about change to the shape of the vagina. Men may find it difficult to cope with their wife's physical and emotional changes and may feel very left out by everything that is going on. The worry for couples is that things will 'always be like this'; it is then easy to lose sight of anticipated pleasure and delight. Couples feel very disturbed if their feelings of 'being in love' are lost as they come under pressure. This is an ideal time to offer support and encouragement to help them to move on.

Sleeplessness

Sleeplessness for the couple starts well before the baby arrives. Pregnancy may bring nausea, anxiety, cramps, haemorrhoids, constipation, foetal movement and increasing difficulty in finding a sleeping position that does not press on a distended abdomen.

Difficulties experienced in the pregnancy will at least alert the couple to the idea that there may be further sleep difficulties after the birth. However, not all disturbed sleep is the product of a baby's crying at night. Parents become exhausted, agitated and anxious, and this in itself will inhibit their normal sleep patterns (Kitzinger 1980). Solutions come from the couple's willingness to adapt to a changing situation and to learn from others.

Sex after the birth

This is another vexed topic and a common problem that couples face after a birth, but one they often have difficulty in raising with the clinician. They may not wish to be seen discussing a subject that does not seem to be within the scope of postnatal services, which focus on the baby and maternal health. The sexual needs of the couple and the father may be judged a low priority. However, couples may have a number of complex issues to be discussed after a birth. The most frequent questions are if and when to recommence sexual activity. There are no definitive answers, but it is helpful if some education is given during pregnancy itself, when the topic may already have been mentioned. A couple may have different expectations of intimacy after the baby is born, but fail to voice them. This is a typical and important cause of problems among couples.

Men and women vary in their attitudes to sex during pregnancy and after childbirth. They may have a variety of fears and reasons to avoid sex. Men who have witnessed the birth may be emotionally affected by it and fearful about a return to sexual intimacy. In the case study on pages 49–50 we describe a father's altered perception of the mother's vagina following a difficult delivery.

Both partners may be less inclined to want sex and may worry that things will never be the same again. Women often lose interest in sex for a time after childbirth. It may be that they hurt too much to feel any interest – there may be soreness or physical problems associated with the delivery; or they are simply too tired – mothers frequently report they are too exhausted to feel any interest in sex. They will be focusing on the baby and possibly trying to manage other children or even a return to work. As we have described, following a traumatic delivery, either parent may find it difficult to resume sexual intimacy. Added to this, attempts to make love are often interrupted by the baby.

Balancing these exceptional physical and emotional needs with a partner's needs for inclusion and intimacy is not easy. Couples need to be flexible and creative, making use of opportunities for time together when they arise. Sex is not just about physical preparedness, but emotional closeness and a readiness for opportunities for privacy.

Contraceptive choices after the birth

At this stage there is public acknowledgement of the couple as a functioning sexual union that will continue after the baby is born. Choices need to be made to reflect the current circumstances of both parents and their need to avoid or delay any further pregnancies. The couple may still be expressing misinformation, for example that breastfeeding is a reliable contraceptive. They may also describe ambivalence about the need to use contraception or the contraceptive method to be used.

These can be difficult choices for couples, particularly when resumption of sexual intercourse may present the parents with fears of a further pregnancy. Couples who have dissonant views about resuming sex or having more children are more likely to experience relationship difficulties. Cultural and religious restraints may not be agreed between the couple or there may be cultural taboos about contraception being discussed when the father is present.

Miscarriage and stillbirth

In our chapter on sick children, we explore the impact of the loss of a child on the partnership. For both parents, the loss of a baby, whether it is early or late in the pregnancy, is a significant bereavement. The health professional may understandably need to address the mother's immediate physical needs, which take precedence over her psychological wellbeing. However, the clinician working with a mother who experiences a miscarriage or stillbirth needs a heightened awareness of the emotional and psychological impact of the loss on the couple. The parents may fail to share their loss with each other or feel unable even to initiate dialogue. The situation may be further complicated by the marginalisation of the father.

Termination of pregnancy

The person most involved in the decision to terminate a pregnancy will be the mother, who may not have involved her partner or may have failed to reach agreement with him. Sadly, there are also situations where the woman agrees to a termination under duress to save the relationship. This may happen, for example, if she already has an established family and becomes pregnant later in the marriage. Husbands may make it clear that they are not prepared to stay in the relationship if another child is born. This can create a painful and very real dilemma for the woman.

Mental health problems in the puerperium

Most couples adjust to a new baby with pride and joy, offering mutual support and affection. However, pregnancy brings physical and hormonal changes which impact on the mother's mood and mental health, and inevitably on the couple's relationship. 'Postnatal blues' are very common and it is easy to reassure couples about how and when they occur. At this time, men may also experience dramatic swings of emotion. For the father there may be grief that the intimacy shared with his partner has changed forever; instead of being the strong shoulder to cry on, he himself may need to express a sense of loss.

Postnatal depression

This is a serious condition, which affects ten to fifteen per cent of women. It starts two to four weeks after the birth and needs to be detected early to prevent distress or even tragedy for the couple. Fathers may not understand what their partner is experiencing and the relationship may suffer. It is not uncommon for relationship difficulties to coexist with postnatal depression, although the cause and effect between the two states is not sufficiently understood. Untreated, depression can lead to problems in the emotional, cognitive and future intellectual development of the baby (Murray et al. 1999).

Puerperal psychosis

A small number of women (0.1–0.2 per cent) become seriously mentally ill after delivery and may need to be treated with their newborns in specialist mother and baby psychiatric units. It is generally accepted that the sooner symptoms of puerperal psychosis appear, the better the prognosis (Kohen 2000). The couple will be able to see each other, but men are not always welcome in these units, where the partners of some patients may have been abusers.

Case study

The registrar in the antenatal clinic saw an anxious young couple, Jill and Mario, for the second time. Jill's blood pressure was raised and although she had promised to rest as much as possible, she nevertheless hoped to continue working until a few weeks before her baby was born. Jill and Mario worked in a family business, which was thriving and expanding. However, they were busy and all hands were needed. Jill's father was unsympathetic about his daughter's need to rest and annoyed with the couple for starting a family so soon. On this second visit her blood pressure was even higher and she had marked oedema. The registrar insisted that she be admitted to hospital and give up her job. She was desperately anxious for the baby and feeling so unwell that she accepted his decision. She responded well to rest, became very focused on her pregnancy, gave up her job and was allowed to return home.

Mario was now the sole breadwinner and was beginning to feel very stressed. His father-in-law remained unhelpful. Jill remained focused on the needs of the pregnancy and less sympathetic to Mario's problems. They again attended the antenatal clinic together and this time the registrar recognised that the relationship had deteriorated and Mario looked exhausted. He took time to discuss how Mario was feeling, how isolated he felt at home and at work, and how overwhelmed he was by the responsibility of earning enough to provide for the couple and the new baby. His guilt discussing himself when Jill and the baby's needs should be paramount was apparent. The registrar was able to reassure him, affirm his importance in the family unit and help Jill to understand and accept his feelings. The couple left the clinic having promised to plan together how to approach her father and suggest he employ a temporary replacement worker. Jill recognised Mario's need to feel included in the pregnancy and recommended various chapters in the books she had been studying with such enthusiasm. She assured him that she planned to resume work, if only part-time.

Case study

The health visitor had seen Mary in the clinic with many minor complaints about her baby. She was surprised by her regular attendance as this was her third child and she seemed to be a very capable mother with a sunny disposition. When she asked Mary if everything was all right at home, Mary became rather quiet and looked downcast. The health visitor gently commented on this and offered some privacy in her office though her time was rather limited. Mary was grateful and confessed that she and her husband, Steve, were arguing a lot and he seemed to have 'gone off her', though she was happy to have sex with him. Steve had been unwilling or unable to be present at the birth of their first two children, but had attended the birth of their third child. This birth had been more difficult than the previous two and Mary had unexpectedly torn. However, everything had healed well and she was settled on the contraceptive pill.

Mary was becoming worried that their relationship was foundering, as she still loved Steve. The health visitor agreed to make a special visit to their home in the following week when Steve would be there. During the visit, while Mary was collecting their daughter from school, she was able to open discussion with Steve. He confessed that he had found the birth distressing and was horrified by the discomfort Mary had experienced. He struggled to find words to express his difficulty in contemplating sexual penetration having watched the birth. He knew Mary was upset with him, but did not know how to approach the problem, particularly as all their friends and family had been pleased he had been at his child's birth. With the health visitor's help he told Mary how he felt and they agreed to talk about it more and to have lots of cuddles without sexual intercourse. The health visitor agreed to see them in the clinic in a month's time, but she got a call to say everything was fine and they had sorted themselves out after more talking and regular cuddling.

Guidelines for good practice

The vast majority of couples want the best for their child and, when invited to work towards that end, will co-operate if supported and listened to with respect. With support and understanding they are capable of generating solutions to the many minor difficulties of the perinatal period.

On the threshhold – fears and fantasies

- Use opportunities in early pregnancy to provide the couple with a chance to talk about their fears of being pregnant or their antipathy towards the idea, if not the reality. Couples need to be given permission to air these feelings, which are not the same as saying that they are asking for a termination. The health practitioner can create opportunities/guide the conversation, to ask 'How do you feel about being pregnant?' Remember to ask Dad as well as Mum.
- Asking the couple about whether the pregnancy was planned, and what method of contraception they were using, if any, may lead to a fuller exploration of ideas about having a baby. Listening for differences between the couple's ideas is important.
- Each will experience loss in the process of change. There may be fearfulness of loss of intimacy, privacy, sexual attractiveness, energy, earning potential and interest in each other. They will need space to look at these issues safely, and to generate other ideas about how these qualities can be regained through parenthood.
- Sensitivity will ensure that information is offered only when the couple are ready to receive it, or specifically request information or an opinion.

During the pregnancy

- Women may start to complain of difficulty sleeping. Couples need to be asked about what they have tried that already works for them. They need practical suggestions about physical care, diet or extra pillows. They need reassurance or permission to sleep in separate beds or rooms during the pregnancy, or they may need help in reaching a solution that meets their joint needs at least some of the time.
- It is good practice to make no assumptions about the relationship between the man or woman accompanying your patient in the waiting room.
- Allow couples to discuss sexual intimacy by raising the subject. Phrases such as 'I wonder if you have any concerns about sex once the baby is born' may be open-ended enough to begin a discussion. By asking what their current practice is and ascertaining that it is safe practice, you give yourself and them the opportunity to reaffirm their behaviour, and help build their confidence in their own partnership.
- You can help them talk about addressing sexual needs in non-penetrative ways if there are worries about intercourse. They will benefit from sharing how they feel and trying to make time to support each other. Both partners need to understand how important physical closeness and cuddling can be, even when intercourse cannot occur.
- Acknowledge and normalise difficulties (without trivialising them) so couples can keep their experience of pregnancy in perspective.
- Domestic violence is a source of considerable anxiety to midwives. If there is no education or training for working with domestic violence, ensure you have the latest information and government guidelines. Seek support from managers. It should be acceptable to ask a question like 'Have you ever felt like hitting each other? Have you ever felt you wanted to hit? Have you ever lost your temper/lost control?' Questions need to be put in a non-judgemental way.
- The Home Office (2000) has advised that education and training in domestic violence should be included into the curricula of all health professionals and has provided some clear recommendations for practice guidance.
- If you feel out of your depth, seek support and guidance from managers, colleagues and supervisors. An up-to-date list of specialist helping agencies should be available to you, see Resource List, p130.
- Clinicians involved with the patient who is seeking a termination have an opportunity to offer support primarily by listening. Many women come with their mind apparently made up. However, there are still opportunities to discover whether the decision has been made and agreed between both partners, to encourage the expression of emotion,

while avoiding taking sides, and allowing the woman or the couple to find their own solutions and ways of moving on.

- Antenatal classes and sessions involving fathers offer opportunities to raise relationship issues and to hear from other parents. Don't be afraid to raise these issues; it is good practice to initiate discussion between the couple at such classes.
- Encourage the couple to prepare for the birth together. This improves communication and empathy between the couple, and prevents the father from being excluded and alienated. The majority of mothers value the presence of their partner at the birth, and fathers have an opportunity to establish an early bond with their child. Murray and Andrews (2000) provide beautiful images of a newborn following the voice and movements of both parents in the first hours after birth.

The postnatal period

- Discussing contraception is for many an opportunity to voice their anxieties and expectations. If this dialogue cannot be encouraged by the clinician, particularly when there are religious or cultural taboos, the mother can be encouraged to discuss this with her partner in the privacy of her own home.
- For many mothers the sleeplessness of pregnancy pales into insignificance compared with the early months and years of a baby's life. The idea of taking turns to 'stay on guard' in a structured and predictable way, for example, gives the other a chance to sleep without guilt or recrimination. The 'give to get' principle, which underpins reciprocity, is easily understood and not beyond the reach of most couples. Books are available on how to 'train' the baby to sleep and sleep clinics can be recommended. Early guidance is invaluable as the initial weeks and months seem to create a good foundation for future management. Remember, no parent will accept advice, however well intentioned or wise, unless they are listened to, empathised with and understood.
- Do not panic when sexual difficulties are mentioned. You can offer a lot of support by giving permission to share problems, by normalising where appropriate and by helping patients work out how to resolve their difficulties. Encourage dialogue and remind them of the importance of closeness and affection without sex.
- Questions about when to resume sexual intercourse may be a plea from the mother for collusion against her partner. Encourage her to share her feelings and fears with her partner. You can help them to see that there is no single right answer, but one that should be talked about until there is a common understanding of what can be expected of each other.
- This is a crucial time to normalise difficulties – not just the physical strains and stresses, but the emotional disturbance and changes in the couple's relationship.

CHAPTER 5

Sick Children – parents under pressure

Introduction

This chapter differs from the rest of the book inasmuch as the patient is the child of the couple. It is well known that a sick child has a profound impact on the family involved; what remains less clear is how that stress affects the partnership of the parents, including their health and wellbeing. In a study exploring the critical events and problems in the eighteen months before respondents approached agencies for help with their marital problems, Brannen and Collard (1982) found that twenty-five per cent of the marriages involved a sick or behaviourally disturbed child.

Parents of sick children face a varied and extensive range of health problems, with disease processes that may have a good prognosis and those that do not. These include acute to chronic sickness, behavioural and developmental difficulties, life-threatening disease, injury, dying and the death of a child.

When we asked clinicians where they met parents coping with their sick children, they described a wide range of settings, from schools and community clinics to specialist paediatric care and hospices. A surprising number of practitioners saw children with minor disabilities, for example, hearing deficits and sight problems, and described their work helping parents to adjust.

Parents of children with chronic disease experience greater stress and burdens than parents of healthy children. Depending on how chronic illness in children is defined, it has been estimated (Midence 1994), that between ten and twenty per cent of children in the UK suffer from chronic illness. However, the impact of childhood chronic illness and its impact on marital function have received limited research attention. Similarly, a search of the literature reveals a lack of suitable means of assessing the impact of minor illness on children and their parents (McKenna and Hunt 1994). Even common disorders cause considerable disruption to the normal roles of the couple, and particularly to the parent who bears primary responsibility for the care of the sick child. Of critical importance to the child's coping are the illness itself, the child's personality, the social environment and the characteristics of the child's family and, in particular, its parents. This chapter considers how couples respond to the crisis of a sick child and how the clinician can help support the parents.

History

Historically, until the end of the nineteenth century, death or serious illness was a common experience within families. Death was associated with childbirth and acute disease; children and parents alike experienced bereavement in the home. All family members were affected, witnessing and interacting with the dying and the dead. It is only since the twentieth century and in the Western world that couples can reasonably expect to have healthy children who will outlive them. Hospital care has done much to alleviate childhood morbidity and mortality; however, problems for the family remain. Until the 1970s sick children were separated from their parents for weeks or even months for hospital treatment. In adulthood, many have continued to suffer the effects of this early emotional trauma. In recent years changes in nursing practice in the UK have become more focused on the emotional needs of the child. Primary care services are also changing as social and health care attempt to become increasingly integrated. These services could be defined as general health/education services, and those that are specialised for the needs of children.

In the twenty-first century, couples face new dilemmas for their children's health involving choice. Now, early discharge of sick children from hospital has become the norm. Children are reunited with their families earlier than adults with comparable medical conditions, although the family, and parents in particular, may not be equally supported. Early discharge may place an overwhelming responsibility for caring on the couple.

This is a very real issue for single parents and parents whose relationship has broken down because of the long-term stresses of coping with a child's health problems. However, in spite of the increase in single-parent families, eighty per cent of dependent children are growing up in a family headed by a couple of whom the majority (ninety per cent) are married. Cappelli et al. (1994) remark that most research on the effect of chronic illness has not focused on the marriage, but rather on the subjective reports of the mother. The situation is compounded when both parents are working, and the burden on working mothers with a sick child remains a major cause of stress (Ferri and Smith 1996). Parents are now consulted about major surgical and medical interventions, and in some cases even demand treatment for a wide range of health issues. Recent debate about the effectiveness and/or risks of the triple MMR injection for infants has fuelled dissent, not only between clinicians, but also between parents.

Later in this chapter, we shall examine in more detail the discrepancies between mothers and fathers in caring for sick children whilst at work, and the emotional toll this places on the entire family.

Rationale

Our rationale for this chapter is that sick children impact on relationships. Where one partner is not involved or where communication has failed, clinic attendance and treatment compliance may become difficult.

Unusually, clinicians working with sick children are well focused on the family and the substantial health gains that can be achieved by working in partnership with parents. Paediatric medicine is one of the few specialities where the individual patient is assessed and treated as part of other systems. Parents are seen regularly with their child and are recognised as active participants in healthcare. Practitioners certainly have many opportunities to address issues for the couple, including that of their relationship. They may recognise the impact of the sickness on the couple, and equally the advantages of a strong partnership between the parents in promoting the child's health. What remains less clear is who is responsible for supporting the couple. Clinicians may be comfortable dealing with child-focused sickness, but be less confident in responding to the needs of a distressed couple.

It is our aim to encourage clinicians to consider the recovery and rehabilitation of the child by proactively addressing the needs of the parents and their relationship. We recognise that many families are challenging or even abusive and may need more help than the clinician can offer. Sadly, there are many unhappy situations where the needs and rights of the child are paramount, and the child must be protected from the parents. (See chapter 10 on how to make a referral to relevant agencies for those couples who are in crisis.)

Special and long-term needs

Much disability, impairment and chronic sickness goes unnoticed because children with long-term illness have limited access to public places for a variety of reasons. Equally unnoticed are the parents who cope on a day-to-day basis. Ievers and Drotar (1996) compared the parents of children with cystic fibrosis with healthy controls and found higher levels of

distress but equally competent parenting behaviour and family functioning.

In a study of twenty couples, Beresford (1994) showed that most parents found the stresses associated with the care of their disabled child to
be 'wide ranging, unrelenting and sometimes overwhelming'. Such
stresses increase the risk of marital breakdown, which is itself a risk factor
in the physical and mental wellbeing of both adults and children
(McAllister 1995). Sanders, Nicholson and Floyd (1997) found that most
couples experiencing significant marital disruption showed signs of marital strain before the birth of a disabled child. In much the same way,
couples becoming parents of normally developing children suffer similar
effects if they have also shown signs of marital strain before the birth.
Further, marital satisfaction and the quality of the parenting alliance are
among the most significant predictors of personal wellbeing and family
adjustment for couples raising children with disability.

Parenting practices have to change in the light of a new diagnosis and
require re-negotiation and mutual decision on the part of the couple to
accommodate to change. Exploratory work with families confirms this.
Wikler (1986) refers to how parents have to regularly readjust their expectations and to the way their family functions as their child develops.
Parents with low levels of family support, high levels of distress and an
avoidant coping style were associated with poor psychological adjustment
to their children's illness.

Beresford (1994) describes a more recent model of caring to help parents 'cope with the daily hassles and long-term strains of caring for a
disabled child'. He encourages parents to be active in the management of
the care of disabled children, rather than being 'passive recipients of an
onslaught of stress'. We would suggest that health professionals have an
important role in preparing parents for such an approach, since the
model implies a level of communication and collaboration that may not
exist in the relationship. Health practitioners will need to be aware that
some groups are more vulnerable because of lack of support. These may
include ethnic minority groups, lone parents, parents with low incomes,
parents with poor physical or mental health, and parents of children with
difficult temperaments or unusual appearance or behaviour.

Loss of a child

The traumatic loss or threatened loss of a child is an exceptional and life-
long emotional challenge to the parents' relationship as a couple. After
the death, the loss will test their capacity to use the relationship for grieving. Cudmore and Judd (2001) use Freud's idea of the 'work of mourning'
as a kind of reality testing. Part of the ability to achieve that will be

determined by how secure the couple have been in their attachment to each other; and partly how they have resolved grief and loss in their individual earlier lives. In their project on bereaved parents, Cudmore and Judd (2001) found that parents could resolve their grief – and that clinicians had a role to play. They quote the analogy made by Bowlby – that the surgeon does not mend bones, but creates conditions that permit bones to heal themselves. They did find that clinicians were anxious about helping couples face their loss. This was related to the complexity and intensity of that loss – likened to an 'internal holocaust' – but also to fears that clinicians had about the impact of such grief on their own emotional wellbeing.

Clinical settings

There is a very wide range of clinical settings for sick children. They may be seen in the community, for example, in 'baby clinics', school medical services, in primary healthcare, acute and long-term hospital settings, hospices, special needs units, mental health units, sexual health departments, young people's services and emergency and social services, to mention just a few. Health professionals also see children at home, with their parents and siblings. Health visitors in particular identify the needs of families where there are children with special needs, and have a role in supporting them. They reported that in many cases they find the mother had almost sole responsibility for everyday care, with the father working outside the home. Differentiated roles, however, did not necessarily mean that the parents were not sharing the additional responsibilities of a sick child – a theme we shall discuss below.

In recent years, the hospice movement has embraced children's services, where health professionals work comprehensively with families and family issues. Specialists can provide an opportunity for the whole family to learn and listen to each other. A clinician we contacted who was working in a children's hospice offering respite care for the family described respite as an opportunity to work with the whole family and, in particular, to support the couple. The hospice invited the family to reside, the sick child was treated, siblings were helped and the parents encouraged to go out as a couple, knowing that their children would be safe.

Paediatric nurses in medical and surgical settings will be involved with parents in making difficult decisions about their child's management and with compliance in treatment, especially when this involves gross changes in their lifestyle, diet and relationships with other family members. Nurses become a key channel of communication between busy medical staff and distressed parents who need to be heard and understood. Opportunities to involve both parents in decisions and care are often made by the health practitioners. This supports US research, which has shown more positive outcomes for children where fathers are more involved in care (One Plus One 2002).

Mental health practitioners, including child psychotherapists, deal not only with sick children, but also with their siblings, who may develop behavioural or emotional disorders. The disturbed behaviour of any of the children in this context may be understood as a communication for the attention of the couple, where the therapist can act as an interpreter to the family. If the couple are themselves struggling with their relationship, they may be seen separately before work with the family can begin.

The role of midwives is becoming more inclusive in the UK. There is a move at present to extend their role to include wider responsibility for women's health. By implication, this means that the midwife will need to consider the woman's partnership, as it impacts on her health (Department of Health 1999).

Emergencies – accidents

We shall deal with life-threatening injury in Chapter 6, 'Trauma'. A child in accident and emergency services poses a unique challenge to the couple. Where one partner is absent, the other may have to make critical decisions about an intervention, and may feel isolated, abandoned and angry. Many couples may draw on deep resources and come closer during a crisis, but there is a tendency to attribute blame either to the self or others after the stress of an accident. Couples who have unfinished business or unresolved conflict, however, are more vulnerable to breakdown during a child's emergency. The incident becomes the final insult to a struggling relationship and poses a special difficulty to overstretched emergency clinical staff.

Couple problems

Many couples cope remarkably well with sick, injured or disabled children, despite the fact that the family has to undergo sometimes very rapid restructuring. Sickness unbalances relationships and may accentuate gender roles. Even parents with a good working relationship will be tested to the full. Relationships that are currently going through a bad patch or that are vulnerable will suffer more when a child becomes ill, and will have to undergo more adjustments.

Communication and negotiation between the couple are key elements in ensuring that these adjustments occur (Clulow and Mattinson 1989; Crowe and Ridley 1990).

Most parents develop patterns or 'templates' for relating to each other and to their children. When a sick child enters the equation, families fall back on these established patterns as a way of managing their lives and any crises that arise. Some couples appear able to adjust and call on their personal resources, support from each other and others around them to cope. Other couples struggle to adapt to even a minor ailment. A good example is the rush of anxious parents and asthmatic infants into accident and emergency hospital departments at night where couples regularly appear to be at loggerheads about when to bring the baby for medical help. The clinical staff may have to focus not only on the child's needs, but also on alleviating the couple's conflict and helping them establish more explicit and shared patterns of managing the next crisis (Parad and Parad 1990; Morrod 2002).

Physical issues

Exhaustion plays a significant role in couples with a sick child, compounded by anxiety, self-neglect and the many additional physical tasks that the couple will need to undertake in addition to their usual responsibilities. Couples may neglect each other as well, with less attention and time spent together. Meals and their preparation deteriorate; the house becomes less comfortable; other children may be sidelined or even become ill themselves. Sexual activity may suffer or cease altogether during a crisis, and sleep and leisure activities will be disrupted. The wider family and work will suffer from the same neglect. Tired, anxious parents become irritable and even aggressive partners.

Finances

Illness is an expensive business. Couples on low incomes and the self-employed may lose overtime pay, hourly wages and opportunities for finding work. Travel to and from hospital is costly – petrol, parking fees or public transport costs all eat into a modest family budget and take up valuable time. Families cannot use that time to prepare meals and so use convenience or take-away food, which costs more. Sick children require medicine, heating, extra toys or treats and the demands of a special diet. The crisis of a sick child undermines the couple's capacity to budget and generate income. Couples may be too anxious or proud to seek the appropriate financial supports that are available, or be unaware of them.

Discipline issues

A sick child presents a unique challenge to the couple. Parenting and disciplining children are never easy. Couples help themselves by sending a clear message of partnership to their children; however, it will be difficult with a sick child to maintain that message. An example of this might be a father who becomes more protective of and indulgent towards a sick child, and a mother who is trying to maintain consistency. Couples are faced with the demands of siblings and the efforts they will make to be heard and understood – possibly by challenging existing rules within the family.

Gender differences

A feature of care for sick children is the way in which fathers are marginalised, not only by their choices in the partnership, but also by health professionals and even health researchers, who omit to inform or consult fathers.

> Fathers became particularly distressed that once they had returned to work many appointments were made with professionals for their wives and children during the time when they were at work. Having constantly to receive anxiety-raising information through their wives was not always a positive factor in the relationship, and caused some fathers to feel that they were, inevitably, the secondary partner. (Herbert and Carpenter 1994)

Others feel like 'the peripheral parent' (Carpenter and Herbert 1994). Typically, fathers' needs were not addressed or even noticed. Worse, they were expected to be the 'supporters', the stronger partner, the competent person in a crisis. As one father described it: 'I returned to work, but in a fog. The feelings of disorientation were enormous and even simple tasks took considerable effort to complete. This only served to disempower me even further.'

At a time when support is desperately needed, parents may find themselves losing closeness. They have different experiences of illness and different ways of struggling to contain their feelings. Each has a different understanding of what has happened to their child, and a notion of what their response should be. They may even 'get it wrong' in their attempts to console and support each other. Many men attempt to support their partners and spare them the burden of their own feelings by remaining emotionally remote. Mothers describe fathers as being reassuring and wanting to move on. In reality, fathers' distress may be so great that they fear being overwhelmed and incapacitated by the depth of their grief, particularly after a bereavement.

Health professionals we have spoken to report that it is mostly mothers who do the main coping at home, whereas they report fathers seem to have more difficulty coming to terms with the child's illness or disability. Typically in chronic illness or special needs, a father may spend much time working outside the home. As suggested many mothers accept this balance willingly, knowing that their partners are making a significant economic contribution. Fear of losing their partner and being abandoned with a sick child, however, may influence some mothers. Clearly, separation may make the situation worse, with loss of income and whatever support and company a partner is able to provide.

Responsibility for sick children

In a large sample of British parents (Ferri and Smith 1996), the role of parenting sick children was explored. Mothers, whether employed full-time or part-time, were always more likely than fathers to agree that it should be the mother who takes time out of work to care for a sick child. They valued the normality of family life. Their fundamental motivation to care came from the pleasure and satisfaction of the relationship with their disabled child. The social construct of the 'good' mother included giving priority to childcare, especially for the very young. Women's endorsement of these social expectations were as strong as their partners'; even in homes where mothers were the sole earners, only two per cent of their unemployed male partners took on the role of care of sick children. Although many women believe this to be the best way of doing things, there is inevitably a stress placed on the relationship, with women's income and wellbeing placed in jeopardy.

Health interventions tend to focus on the identified patient, whereas a more useful intervention might be to help the couple use their own resources within everyday family life. The clinician working in partnership with parents will respect their decisions and choices for arranging their domestic lives, help them to test the reality of their choice and create opportunities for expressing emotions – both positive and negative. They may have a role to play in encouraging common understanding/education of the extended family and of discouraging them from taking sides with either spouse.

The other children

The birth order of the sick child will impact on the response of the family and siblings and the differing responsibilities of family members. Coping with the needs of a sick child or a child with special needs may lead unavoidably to neglect of siblings. Many couples agonise about the unmet needs of their other child or children. Others may be unaware and too engrossed with the sick child to notice or understand. Their burdens may be increased if siblings 'act out' – behaving badly or developing physical symptoms or becoming emotionally disturbed. Siblings may feel guilty or resentful and be unable to express their underlying emotions.

Case study

Bill arrived at casualty with his six-year-old daughter Megan, who was having breathing difficulties, and with his four-year old son in tow. Megan has a history of asthma, which had been well controlled with the support of the asthma nurse at their primary care centre, until the last few months. After providing treatment, the junior doctor asked about known precipitants of the attack, and Bill confessed that there had been a family row. On further questioning, he reported that he and his wife had had a noisy argument that afternoon, following his late arrival home. He explained that his wife had been made late for her work shift for the third time in a month, and had accused him of selfishness. Bill became tearful as he talked.

The doctor suspected at this stage that Megan's attacks were connected to the marital distress and decided to spend a little more time with Bill. She heard that his wife had been very critical since she returned to work and he felt defensive and unfairly accused. For his part, Bill had been very busy at work, but found it difficult to finish work to strict time boundaries. He also described difficulty handling his son, who had become uncooperative and withdrawn. They had had many unresolved arguments about their new roles, some of which had been witnessed by the children. The doctor acknowledged his guilt, his hurt and the difficulty of having a sick child. She normalised his experience by pointing out the challenge facing all couples who are working parents. At this point, Bill recognised that he and his wife had not talked through their new roles and responsibilities, nor had they supported each other and considered the impact of unresolved conflict on their children. The doctor encouraged him to return to the practice nurse for ongoing support and work on their family difficulties.

Case study

Aneega, a lively fifteen-year-old, was admitted to an oncology unit of a district general hospital, following a diagnosis of leukaemia. Her prognosis was good and had been shared with her parents, who no longer live together. Aneega lives with her mother and two sisters and sees her father and his new partner at least twice a month. Aneega's greatest worry is that her treatment will interfere with her school work and that she will not be able to go to college and pursue higher education. Her mother is more concerned about her general health and Aneega's capacity to comply with the treatment that the hospital will be offering. Her father is anxious as his new partner is expecting their first child and is fearful of losing contact with his daughter at this critical time in her life.

The very different agendas resulted in the family expressing a lot of anxiety and anger when first seen by the ward staff. Aneega became tearful and accused both parents of being selfish and uncaring. Her parents in turn blamed themselves and each other in equal measure. They expressed their grief and guilt by blaming each other first, which perpetuated the row, whereupon Aneega left the room, weeping and distressed.

At this point, the nurse specialist who was conducting the interview suggested to Aneega's father that he went and 'rescued' his daughter and reassured her that whatever differences there might have been, that both parents were concerned for Aneega's full recovery and wellbeing. He did so and Aneega was reluctantly brought back into the room.

The clinician highlighted the differing but legitimate desires of the whole family. She especially encouraged Aneega's father in his continued support of his daughter and his involvement in her education. She suggested to the couple that all of these worries had been heard by the staff and could be addressed during Aneega's stay. She also invited Mum and Dad, if they were willing, to have some additional time to see her, perhaps when Aneega was seeing her ward tutor. This provided Aneega and her parents with enough respite to accept that they could work together, and indeed had to work together, if they were all to survive Aneega's illness.

Guidelines for good practice

- Clinicians who work with sick children have an opportunity to value the experience of the couple. Keep communication lines open with the family from the very first day.
- Meet the couple on their own if practical, but accept the absence of one parent if necessary.
- Listen and provide opportunities to talk.
- Normalise if appropriate, but be careful not to trivialise their experience. Demonstrate sensitivity to the particular couple. Each couple's experience is unique. Comparison with other parents or groups is rarely helpful – especially if there are attempts to minimise suffering through comparisons.
- Accept the feelings the couple have for the child and stay with their genuine experience. Give permission to express hostile or ambivalent feelings towards the child.
- Give couples permission to seek normality. Provide a safe place for anger and blame. If the couple is planning further pregnancies, ensure they receive good genetic counselling if appropriate.
- The first resource that couples request is more information about their child and the illness or injury that has occurred, both as a way of making sense of what has happened and for planning the future. Couples

need time to work out 'why us?' and to give vent to feelings of being victimised or stigmatised.

- Support includes giving good information, including relevant web-sites and library resources. The extended family may benefit if well informed.
- Create a flexible timetable for grieving, education and talking to each other about the sick child. Correct misinformation.
- Ascertain the couple's understanding of their child's condition. Look for inconsistencies or misinformation between the couple and their notes, and between partners, and correct them.
- Clinicians working with couples who have a sick or injured child might like to provide information to the couple about self-help groups. Self-help is not an alternative to care, but can be offered as part of ensuring that the couple have access to as many resources as possible during the adjustment they are both making to their new roles within their family. We have listed some of the better known organisations in the Resource List at the end of this book, but we do recognise that there are limitations. Some couples see them as amateur or as stigmatic, and not all families want to share or network with others in similar circumstances. It remains the case that many couples may continue to see a health professional as the more valid source of support and information.
- Demonstrate respect for the child; visit the child and use her/his name. Can you identify a positive attribute? Avoid medical/diagnostic jargon, for example, 'Debbie suffers from epilepsy'; not 'Debbie is an epileptic'.
- Establish what the team policy is about breaking bad news, and agree it with colleagues.
- Be available at periods of health and development transition.
- Ask how they have dealt with sickness in the past and remind them of how they have coped before or helped others to cope.
- Respect gender differences. Beware of forming alliances with one partner whose behaviour you find more credible or appropriate. Work with each partner in different ways. Encourage the idea of a team which has to establish a working alliance, for example, he works long hours and earns; she works long hours with the child. Remember that there is no need to share every experience or activity! Help couples to accept and understand the different experience of their partner, but accept also that if the difference becomes a burden to the couple, they may require referral to a couple counsellor.
- Help them to keep a balance – each family member has competing needs.
- Help couples deal with marital conflict, poverty, recent bereavement or other young children – these may be a greater source of distress than the sick child, and may also require further help.
- You may be in a position to help them understand issues around child discipline, protecting the child or overprotection.

- Allow the couple to decide if, when and where they feel they have a problem, and when they need outside assistance. It is very important to stay with a couple's distress without recourse to activity or referral. Clinicians often have to resist the temptation of being too active as a way of coping with their own impotence or distress.
- You may find yourself dealing with excessive drinking and extramarital affairs, drugs, depression or anger. Care for yourself by seeking good supervision and support. Be clear about your personal and professional boundaries and protocol for staff protection.

Bereavement

The loss of a child ranks as highest among events that induce the severest grief, stress or breakdown. Couples who are bereaved share the experience described by all close observers of grief (Murray Parkes 1986; Young and Papadatou 1997). There are recognised bereavement processes that need to be understood by the clinician and eventually by the couple. Shock and a sense of devastation at the event; denial that the event is about to or has actually happened; anger and a desire to attribute blame to someone or something that has made this event happen; and, finally, acceptance of the event and the beginning of grief. These experiences do not necessarily follow in temporal sequence, and may occur simultaneously, or not at all. For some couples, there is no resolution for their grief.

Carol Werlinich, Director of the Family Service Center, Maryland, conducted extensive telephone interviews with forty mothers who had experienced the violent loss of a child (Werlinich 2001). These families constitute an at-risk group who have special needs in therapy. The mothers strongly underlined the importance of listening and almost shouted a list of don'ts for clinicians to keep in mind:

- Don't try to 'fix it'.
- Don't say you understand.
- Don't expect them to 'feel better' – it gets 'softer', not 'better'.
- Don't do anything but listen to their pain. Don't be afraid of mothers' pain and don't rush them.
- Don't remind them of what they already know – that they have other family and children alive, for example.
- Don't make the mistake of believing that existing or future children can replace a loss.
- Don't be shocked at suicidal thoughts – these may be not so much a plan to kill oneself, as a wish not to be alive.
- Don't be surprised at how differently partners grieve or how the relationship might be suffering. Fathers are often overlooked in grief.
- Don't be alarmed at very frequent trips to the cemetery, or none at all; everyone's grief is expressed differently.

Chapter 6

Trauma – injuring the relationship

Introduction

Historically, it was only in the twentieth century that the psychological impact of trauma was framed as a health issue. Shell-shocked soldiers in World War I were the first to receive medical care for their condition. At the beginning of the twenty-first century, there is debate about compensation for policemen, firefighters and soldiers with physical and mental scars of life-threatening events acquired in the course of their duties.

In everyday language, the term 'trauma' has become synonymous with 'stress' as in 'she had a traumatic day when she lost her air ticket'. In medicine the term trauma refers to 'an injury or wound violently produced'. Most medical texts define 'trauma' in terms of type of injury and its impact on the individual's physical function. In psychiatry it refers to 'an emotional experience or shock that has a lasting psychic effect'.

This last, formal definition of trauma refers not just to violence, but to the effect of that violence on the victim, and both imply that the effect endures.

The meaning that the patient attaches to the injury will influence the emotional response, the severity of symptoms and the speed and effectiveness of recovery. As Clulow and Mattinson (1989) observe, 'tragedies affect different people in different ways, depending on how the person perceives what has happened to him, and how that perception reverberates on his inner world'. Suffering does not take place in a vacuum, but only in relation to a particular life history (Williams 1972). We would add the quality of the patient's partnership to the equation.

Rationale

Trauma medicine focuses on restoring the individual's functioning. It less often concerns itself with the impact of such events on partners and other family members, who may also have experienced the trauma, whether directly or indirectly. This chapter explores the impact on the couple when one or both, or their immediate family has faced life-threatening injury, involving intense fear. It will also guide the clinician in counselling them in recovery and rehabilitation. Clinicians who have access to both the victim and partner are uniquely placed to support the couple in understanding and sharing their experience and recovering from it together more quickly (McFarlane and Bookless 2001; Mills 2001). Treatment of trauma symptoms needs to address the fact that the effect of trauma not only alters relationships, but also can be regulated by relationships. This raises the question of whether or not to use interpersonal psychotherapy for the treatment of traumatised patients and their partners. Although developed for the treatment of depression, positive results have been demonstrated in the treatment of post-traumatic stress disorder (PTSD) by interpersonal psychotherapy (Krupnick, Green and Miranda 1998).

Basic coping patterns to change and to loss will also apply to the couple's capacity to respond to trauma. Couples who communicate effectively, who are flexible in their roles, who are essentially optimistic and who have a family and a wide circle of friends are more likely to cope with the overwhelming experience of trauma. In contrast to this, poor education, limited social contacts, poverty and poor mental and physical health have all been identified as contributing to the stress of injury and its impact on the couple's relationship. The circumstances of the injury and its meaning to the couple, however, are also likely to be a significant factor in the capacity to respond and recover. The presence of litigation or other judicial processes may also have a bearing on outcome.

We are aware that couples face sudden changes in their lives in the context of other illnesses, such as when their survival and wellbeing are threatened; their responses have been described in other chapters. This chapter will consider traumatic contexts for the couple who have experienced violence, and some of the problems that arise for the couple during and after trauma. The rationale of this chapter is to alert clinicians to the need to help maintain communication after life-threatening events. Clinicians can also help the couple help each other before seeking specialist help or referral.

Clinical settings

Trauma may feature in any health setting. Accident and emergency departments receive critically injured and walking wounded, but of course patients and their partners are then referred to appropriate medical and surgical hospital wards, or seen in follow-up outpatient clinics, as well as in primary care settings. Once the physical injury is treated, and the patient is well on the way to recovery, the patient and partner begin to reveal their distress to the clinician in any setting where they believe they will be heard. It is just as likely to be a physiotherapist or occupational therapist who will be the first to hear the psychological sequelae of trauma and its impact on the couple. This will include mental health settings, where patients with severe anxiety or depression after injury are referred for psychiatric treatment.

Patients suffering trauma will be seen in midwifery following serious perinatal incidents, for example, following a major haemorrhage. In the aftermath of caring for mother and baby, it is possible to overlook the impact of such an event on the parents' relationship. The much longed-for baby becomes a potential life-threat to the mother and therefore a source of ambivalence for the father.

General practitioners or community nurses see patients who persist in presenting with a variety of anxiety problems. These often appear as physical ailments such as sleeplessness and may be causally linked to a traumatic incident, including medical procedures. These problems interfere with their everyday functioning, including their partnership. In all these settings, the symptoms may be severe enough for a diagnosis of post-traumatic stress disorder (PTSD) to be made.

Post-traumatic stress disorder (PTSD)

In the specific context of post-traumatic stress disorder, The Diagnostic and Statistical Manual of Mental Disorders, DSM-IV (American Psychiatric Association 1994), which is widely used in UK mental health, defines 'trauma' fairly narrowly. An individual must have experienced an event as defined thus:

> The person has been exposed to a traumatic event in which both of the following are present: (1) the person experienced, witnessed or was confronted with an event or events that involved actual or threatened death or serious injury, or a threat to the physical integrity of self or others; (2) the person's response involved intense fear, helplessness or horror (pp. 427(8)).

In this definition a person who was seriously injured but did not have this subjective response would not be deemed traumatised. There are three characteristics of a traumatic response. The first is intrusive symptoms, for example, unwanted thoughts and memories about the event, or dreams, nightmares and flashbacks, where the individual relives the terror of the moment again and again, but is unable to achieve any resolution of it. Typically, the affected person attempts distraction, disclosure or avoidance to keep the symptoms at bay – usually without success. At worst, intrusive symptoms will interfere substantially with everyday living and personal relationships.

The second of these is hyperarousal, where the individual experiences extreme vigilance, for example, constant listening and looking for danger, sleep disturbance, irritability, aggression and poor concentration. The individual recognises at a rational level that the threat has passed, but is physically and emotionally geared for battle and remains unable to relax. Medication, sedation and alcohol may have been tried to reduce arousal, often with variable outcome – for example, alcohol can make an aggressive person more disinhibited and more prone to express anger.

The third characteristic is avoidance, where the individual consciously or unconsciously resists contact with any activity, place or person reminiscent of the trauma, or where the victim believes that memories might occur. Examples include refusing to use a certain route to work, avoiding watching television news and crime thrillers, or talking to anyone who might discuss the event and remind the victim of the injury. A more extreme avoidance response entails the individual being unable to use public transport or to return to work or study, or even staying at home all day without outside contact. Avoidance and social withdrawal can be seen as ways of coping with an overwhelming threat, and afford the sufferer some immediate relief from distress. Individuals can have some or all of the above experiences. The majority of individuals spontaneously recover after a few weeks; a minority do not and go on to develop PTSD. Victims attempt to make sense of impossible situations and struggle alone, often finding it easier to blame themselves or sometimes becoming aggressive towards their partner or children because the enemy is no longer there.

Accidental injuries

Trauma victims who have been in accidents or natural disasters will be treated for their injuries and may well be offered counselling soon after the incident. There is some evidence to show that immediate debriefing is not therapeutic (McFarlane and van der Kolk 1996) and for this reason many services now wait for up to eight weeks before any psychological work is done with victims to allow for spontaneous recovery. Where there is more than one victim, they may be seen as a couple, family or group to help them make sense of what has happened and to provide each other with information and support.

Confusion may be present for health practitioners where there is litigation or claims for compensation. When supporting a couple after an accident, it is possible that the injured party may withhold or distort the picture, unknown to the partner, or even collude with the partner against medical staff.

Couple problems

Intimacy is heavily influenced by exposure to trauma. As Mills and Turnbull (2001) observe, 'Trauma exacerbates the fear of losing hard-won, deeply connected relationships which are so precious to most people.' Intimacy that has been lost as the result of trauma is potentially undermining to the couple: 'Functions of the mind that spoil what we call "intimacy" will deepen and darken the "black hole of trauma"' (van der Kolk and McFarlane 1996). Some couples are able to rise to the challenge without support; others are less successful.

Life-threatening injury brings the couple, possibly for the first time, close to the emotional challenge that death, loss or near-loss creates. A key issue here for the couple is that partners are intrinsically unique and may respond quite differently to threat. The differences are determined by a wide range of factors. Each partner in the relationship will attach different meaning to the traumatic event; each will have had different emotional experiences; and each will devise a different coping strategy to survive. In addition, the effect on each partner is mediated by more general conditions. These include *pre-traumatic* factors, such as past personal and family psychiatric history, socio-economic status (SES) (low SES is associated with higher risk) and gender, with women more vulnerable. *Peri-traumatic* factors include the type of injury, the level of danger perceived at the time of the injury and the rapid onset of depression which causes substantial damage to a couple's intimacy. *Post-traumatic* factors (where the clinician has most to contribute) include lack of social support, the outcome of trauma on the couple's financial circumstances and the degree of that loss. Secondary stressors include the increasing distancing and isolation of the couple from each other.

Response to trauma is comparable to that of grief, that is, the individual and the couple face the processes of shock, followed by denial, anger and adjustment to perceived or actual loss. Injury that entails the death of others, and then leads to one's own loss of function, chronic ill health, loss of job, status, appearance and friends, can be shared and resolved within a loving family and, in particular, within the partnership.

Couples not able to listen to each other at this critical time will evolve separate strategies for coping. These may be in direct opposition to each other. For example, a victim of a road traffic accident coped by describing the events to everyone in graphic detail; the spouse, however, had managed to cope with the possibility of becoming a widow by trivialising the accident and making light of his experience. Such a disparity led to arguments and loss of faith in each other, disrupting intimacy and future plans.

What is clear is that injured parties do not always share their distress with their loved ones. Couples who have poor communication patterns pre-trauma are more likely to withhold information post-trauma. In a

study of 300 couples, Mills (2001) found that, where one party had PTSD
or secondary traumatisation, ninety per cent were unable to share their
grief with the partner. This placed their relationship more at risk of failing
to resolve the traumatic stress. These people gave the following reasons:

- fear of overburdening the partner
- fear of lack of sympathy or not been listened to
- fear that partner could not manage intense reactions
- fear of loss of respect from partner
- fear of losing partner when 'the whole truth was known'
- fear of partner sharing with others not approved of by the victim
- anxiety that partner would remember the trauma too long
- concern about 'contamination' of the family by traumatic memories
- fear that partner would use perceived weakness to gain power in the
  relationship
- anxiety about criticism from partner for poor coping pattern.

Victims compartmentalised their relationship and, in many cases,
idealised it to the point where it could not be spoiled by traumatic mem-
ory. Some war veterans saw their marriages as 'safe havens' where their
spouses' ignorance of their experiences was misjudged by veterans to be
a desirable state of affairs.

Victims of war and civil disaster

There are many people – both combatant and non-combatant – who work
in dangerous occupations and who are themselves prepared in some measure for disaster. These include the armed forces, police, building and
engineering personnel, emergency workers, transport workers, mariners
and journalists. Their partners and families, however, are not as well prepared and suffer significant levels of anxiety. Hall and Simmonds (1973)
reported a wide range of psychological and psychosomatic problems experienced by wives enduring enforced separation from their soldier husbands.
These included spastic colitis, migraine, cervical collar pain, asthma, cardiac
neurosis and gastrointestinal symptoms. Further studies by McCubbin,
Hunter and Dahl (1975) confirm the significant effect on partners and children. Others who are bystanders of such events are more vulnerable and
suffer more as a consequence. These include the civilian populations in war
and the witnesses of disaster. Overall, the experience of disaster appears to
be linked to the level of control victims have over the incidents.

Victims of war who have been raped as an act of war have complex
reasons for not sharing their experiences with others. Individuals subjectively report shame, guilt, fear of rejection by the partner and, in some cultures,
a sense of having been forever sullied by the enemy. There remains in the

minds of both parties a sense that 'things will never be the same again'.

In general, rape survivors and their partners face a great challenge. The patient not only suffers the attack, but the internal turmoil of many questions, some unspoken. Questions both partners ask include:

- Why didn't you protect me?
- Why did you put yourself at risk?
- Why are all men so evil?
- Why do you generalise about men?
- Can I face sex again?
- Will you let me love you again?
- Is she exaggerating?
- Does he believe me?

Survivors of torture

Patients who have been unfortunate enough to suffer torture may have to contend with losses including their beliefs about the world being a safe place; loss of their homeland; or loss of job and social and economic support. Their difficulties are compounded when the victim has not disclosed to the other the details of their suffering. In some cases, both partners have endured torture separately and again they will be reluctant to share with the other the full nature of their suffering. The 'wall of silence' can create other difficulties, sexual and mood disorders being the most common.

Crime

Victims of crime, including those who suffer sexual crimes and domestic violence – i.e. from their sexual partner – have further difficulties. These include disclosure, ongoing safety, criminal proceedings and their consequences and, above all, a betrayal of trust. In the UK it has been estimated that one in four families experience domestic violence in their lifetime. In general, the majority of victims are still women, and men the perpetrators. In the US violence between partners causes more injury than road accidents, muggings and rapes put together: six million women are injured and 4,000 are killed by their partners annually. In Canada half of all women in a nation-wide survey over the age of sixteen years have experienced violence from their partners, and one in ten was in fear of her life (Statistics Canada 1993; Kershaw et al. 2000; d'Ardenne and Balakrishna 2001). There is, therefore, the same probability that you as a clinician will be facing this type of trauma with the couples that you see in general health settings.

Help-seeking for victims of domestic violence is variable. There is evidence that older women married to their abusers are less likely to seek help, and express most helplessness, economic dependence, embarrassment, shame and self-blame than their unmarried, younger and more confident sisters. Men report partner abuse much more often and are least likely to blame themselves for violence received. Furthermore, they do not perceive violence as the inevitable price of intimacy (McFarlane and van der Kolk 1996). Women are more likely to reveal this kind of violence to health workers than to the police, and will actively select a clinician whom they think will believe them.

Trauma and its effect on sexuality

There is a wide literature describing the significant effect of sexual injury, including childhood sexual abuse, rape and sexual torture, on subsequent sexual function (Fieldman-Summers, Gordon and Maegher 1979; Becker et al. 1986). For women, the most common effects are loss of libido, anorgasmia, sexual phobias, avoidance of intimacy and vulnerability, which can affect the relationship beyond intimacy. For men, the effects include erectile difficulties, finding sex boring and/or burdensome, pain during intercourse (dyspareunia) and plummeting loss of desire. There is little doubt that the profound effects of life-threatening events impact not just on intimacy, but also on specific sexual function. However, it is unlikely that sexuality will be an initial priority for the clinician or the patient, although the effect on the couple may be devastating.

Victims vary in their response. Ehlers and Clark (2000) describe 'mental defeat' as a major factor determining post-traumatic reaction, including self-image. If victims see themselves as not coping and ineffective, they are more likely to see themselves as unattractive sexually, even when there is no physical disfigurement.

De Silva (2001) reviewed the effect of non-sexual trauma on sexuality and found it to be complex and interactive. Direct injury and pain, as well as restriction of movement, can lead to loss of sexual function as well as associated loss of body image and self-esteem. For example, soldiers who had a limp or a temporary colostomy reported a damaged sense of their sexual self. Patients who are psychologically traumatised experience depression, guilt and anxiety, and this directly affects their sexual drive and performance. De Silva (2001) quotes Solomon: 'sexual problems may compound the difficulties that PTSD veterans have in maintaining intimate contact with their wives. Not a few PTSD veterans report a drastic curtailment of sexual activity to the point of complete abstinence.' Any reader should note, however, that not all traumatised patients have sexual dysfunction; clearly pre-trauma factors will also have a bearing on outcome and more studies are needed in this important field.

Couples can be very resourceful, especially with guidance from a sympathetic clinician. The following case studies describe problems involving a skilled intervention from a clinician who was not a trained counsellor.

Case study

Jane witnessed a late-night attack on her partner Jerry who sustained serious chest wounds requiring surgery and intensive care. Jerry started rehabilitation, but Jane became increasingly anxious and unable to go anywhere near the street where he had been attacked. This was a problem because it was very close to their home and made leaving the house for work increasingly difficult. The occupational therapist recognised early on that there were two victims of this attack and decided to invite both parties to talk about their fears. She explained the effect of violence on both of them, and how avoidance of feared situations was proving to be an ineffective strategy for dealing with the aftermath of trauma. Jerry was recovering from his physical wounds but Jane had post-traumatic stress difficulties. With the help of the occupational therapist, Jerry and Jane planned a graded behavioural programme, which would allow the couple to use each day together, walking closer and closer to the street where Jerry was nearly murdered. Jerry would talk to Jane about the planned visit first, and they would agree in some detail how and when they would tackle their visit. This gave Jane the chance to practise the visit in her mind (cognitive rehearsal) and begin to face her fear in her imagination. Then they visited the street in the daytime until she could walk in it with Jerry without panicking. Later they progressed to evening and night visits and, although Jane did not enjoy these walks, both realised that she had faced her fears. She was no longer avoiding the street and allowing the attack to interfere with their lives.

Case study

Following a road traffic accident Patrick was referred by his doctor to the local physiotherapy service to help with non-specific pain. During assessment, he appeared anxious and aggressive, and complained that since the accident, he had begun to argue with his partner Sean without provocation. During therapy, Patrick was able to tell his physiotherapist about the effects of the accident on his relationship. He described how they were unable to enjoy sex, and that the constant irritability was interfering with their sleep and Patrick's physical and emotional recovery. At the suggestion of the physiotherapist, they both joined their local sports centre and registered for adult swimming classes. As Patrick learnt to swim, he increased his stamina and self-confidence. He was also able to vent some of his pent-up aggression safely into the physical activity. Sean also learnt to swim better and improved his self-esteem and sense of fun. Swimming was not the solution to their difficulties, but it represented a point of change when they could safely talk about their difficulties. As a consequence, they were able to face their insecurities and generate some shared ideas about tackling them together.

Case study

Serena is a Kosovan woman who was raped and beaten by soldiers in her village during the Balkan war while her husband Etmond was in hiding in the mountains. They recognised that the attack was intended to punish both of them for Etmond's political activities and to try and lure him from hiding. Two years later, they sought asylum in the UK. Serena began to show many gynaecological symptoms, and was seen in her local department of gynaecology with non-specific urethritis as well as serious signs of depression. The marriage was now under considerable strain, and Serena was unwilling to discuss the rape with Etmond. She blamed her husband for the attack, as well as for failing to protect her. She even blamed him for choosing the losing side in the conflict. Serena was torn between seeing her husband as a co-victim and seeing him and all other men in the conflict as perpetrators. Etmond expressed shame and helplessness, but wanted to talk. The clinician recognised Serena's extreme distress and engaged the couple with the idea of a joint referral to their community mental health team.

Guidelines for good practice

Good practice involves education about the impact of trauma on the individual and also on the relationship. Couples need to feel that they have something in common with the rest of the world and that they are not isolated. It will be very frightening to live with someone who, overnight, has become irritable, aggressive, uncommunicative and unable to sleep or concentrate. The couple are capable of understanding that these post-traumatic signs are how the individual tries to make sense of what is incomprehensible – namely, a life threat.

The practitioner may find that by the time the couple turn for help, they are struggling to adapt to the change in their relationship. This transitional phase gives all three an opportunity to establish a new alliance. The patient's recovery and future wellbeing are critically linked to their personal relationship and maintenance of intimacy.

Scott (1999) has made a number of specific recommendations for counsellors working with traumatised patients, which we have adapted to the needs of the couple and to which we have added some principles ourselves:

• Acknowledge the patient's and the partner's distress. Ensure that there is a common understanding of what each partner has experienced. For example, 'What went through your mind at the moment of impact? What was your worst feeling/physical sensation?' Or for the partner, 'What went through your mind the moment you heard he had been taken to hospital?'

- Education. Explain to the couple the way trauma affects the individual and the partner. For example, you can help the couple with the patient's irritability by first explaining that it is a part of hyper-vigilance in direct response to the trauma.
- Allow the couple to express powerlessness and reassure them that anger is understandable at this stage. Legitimise feelings that are normally seen as taboo. Respect their boundaries. Your patient and partner will tell you if and when they want to talk and what they want to describe. This may be the right time to let the couple know that you value their relationship and the support they give to each other, and that talking about it may be part of the healing process.
- Listen. The clinician can offer the patient and partner the time and opportunity to express their depression, anxieties and sense of failure.
- Help both partners acknowledge that they are processing their trauma and grief in their separate ways. Encourage the couple to stay engaged with each other and available to each other for support.
- Prioritise. It is inappropriate to focus on sexual counselling if the patient is facing depression or PTSD. The couple may be dealing with financial ruin as the result of injury. The clinician responds to these challenges in a timeframe that the couple can engage with. She can advise the couple about priorities and reassure them that intimacy will not be forgotten but dealt with later.
- Provide opportunity for the couple to work out ways of facing injury and its aftermath together. For example, if the patient is continuing to have bad dreams about a trauma, the partner who shares a bed will also be woken and can help the patient to recall the dream, talk about it and make better sense of it.
- Reframe the trauma. Help the couple to move towards seeing themselves as survivors, not victims of trauma. The partner may eventually help the patient to reconstrue the world as a fundamentally safe place. Trauma patients who may have responded with presence of mind, courage or even heroism may nevertheless feel they were ineffective or be ashamed of their injuries. Ask the couple, 'Is there another way of thinking about what happened to you?' At this stage patients are often able to generate an alternative account of the trauma.
- Encourage the couple to move on and plan for the future. Taking up a new and shared creative activity is one option regularly chosen by survivors and their partners. Couples left with anger or a sense of injustice can transform it into a campaign or self-help movement, which can be shared together and with others.

CHAPTER 7

Mental Health – two minds together

Introduction

Mental health and its interaction with the couple relationship historically has been a neglected topic. A leading journal of sexual and marital therapy admitted that in the whole of the 1990s, it had published only four papers in the field of couples and serious mental disorder (d'Ardenne and McCann 1997). Yet nearly fifty per cent of the population of the UK will be affected by poor mental health at some time in life. Partly as a result of this, the National Health Service has reorganised its local services into acute care, primary care and mental health, in an attempt to address the huge mental health need. Depression and other mood disorders are among the most common reasons for people visiting their family doctors, and the greater proportion of the NHS budget is absorbed by psychiatric inpatient care and medication. Kaplan (1992) cites one per cent of the population world-wide as suffering from schizophrenia – an illness that has a devastating effect on interpersonal and social relationships, as well as on libido (Bancroft 1989).

The impact on family and intimate relationships is incalculable. Despite the lack of good information about the role of partners in mental health, we share the view of Cutrona (1996):

> Even though only one individual is sick, the illness is a threat to both partners, and both must make many adjustments in their lives. Thus, both members of the couple experience an increased need for social support, and both members are hampered in their efforts to provide support by the physical and emotional demands of the illness.

Readers will be inspired by Ted Hughes' Birthday Letters to his wife, Sylvia Plath, in which his theme is often the support of the couple for each other during physical and mental illness (Hughes 1998).

Our capacity to form and maintain committed intimate sexual relationships is an important index of good mental health. When one partner becomes ill, the other may be asked to help provide additional information. It is much rarer that the needs of the partner are considered in assessment or healthcare planning. But as a SANE poster so succinctly observes, 'You don't have to have mental illness to suffer from it' (SANE 2000).

Rationale

In chapter 2 we wrote about the role of marriage and committed relationships in the maintenance of physical and mental wellbeing, and the significant correlation between poor intimate relationships and illness. This is especially true in mental health, where the role of the partner in maintaining symptoms or in helping to ameliorate them is critical. The mental health consequences of relationship disruption are well researched. Widowers, for example, have a higher mortality rate, occurrence of mental disorder and tendency to suicide than have widows or married people (Berado 1970). Men who are in the process of separation or divorce are much more likely to suffer from stress-related illness (Bloom, Asher and White 1978). Dissatisfied marital partners are more likely to suffer depression (Weiss and Aved 1978). People in disturbed relationships tend to have higher incidences of low self-esteem, depression, sleep disorders, alcoholism, drug dependence and admission to psychiatric hospital (Duck 1991). Women who have a close relationship with their husband are less likely to suffer postpartum depression (Paykel et al. 1980). Coyne and Downey (1991) have shown a clear link between depression and marital distress, both as a cause and consequence. Brown and Harris (1978) showed that distress was less likely to turn into clinical depression in women if spouse support was available. Where depression does develop, irritability, self-loathing, lack of motivation and intense misery become highly aversive to spouse and family.

This chapter will include a description of the needs of the couple with mental health problems and examples of good practice for clinical staff. Consideration will be given to community aftercare and the role of the community mental health team/outreach team/crisis services in supporting the partner and increasing compliance with health care. We shall talk about couples where one or both have long-term mental health needs, and where the social and relationship needs of the couple have yet to be addressed.

Clinical settings

The vast majority of mental health care in the UK is done with the support of the general medical practitioner (family doctor) and community mental health nurses (or CPNs – community psychiatric nurses).

Referral can be made to secondary or even tertiary mental health care, not necessarily only if health problems become more severe, but also because a carer, often a partner, cannot manage a particular symptom. This can include the risk of self-harm, or the deteriorating mental or physical wellbeing of the patient's partner or family. Families carry high levels of psychiatric morbidity (Jacobson 1994), but the straw that breaks the camel's back is often surprisingly light. An increasingly important role for the health professional has been ensuring that carers' assessments are carried out in a timely fashion and that relapse prevention is a key aim in the care of any mentally ill patient in the community.

Primary care

What distinguishes the family doctor setting from other health settings is that it is the patient who has to decide whether he or she is ill. We share the view of others, however (Holmshaw and Hillier 2000), that illness is a continuum, not a decision between clear health or the absence of it. Indeed, there are many social, cultural and interpersonal factors that will determine when and how a patient seeks help. Mental health problems are a good example of this. When does grief become depression? When does occupational stress become a chronic anxiety state? In primary care, patients range from those described as the 'worried well' to those suffering from major psychosis. The decision to seek help can be influenced in either direction by whether or not a person feels supported, loved and esteemed by significant others.

In a classic study on depression, Brown and Harris (1978) found that the presence of a close, confiding relationship with a husband or partner significantly reduced the risk of women developing clinical depression after a major loss or disappointment, and could therefore be managed within primary healthcare. In comparison, women who were living alone, who did not feel supported or who had a hostile partner were much more likely to come to the attention of medical and social services. Such women did not necessarily complain of poor support. More typically, they presented to their family doctor expressing guilt, low self-worth and a desire to harm themselves or their small children (Kohen 2000).

There are other factors affecting mental disorder in primary care. In poor, inner city areas, the proportion of people with serious mental health problems is directly affected by unemployment, racism, family breakdown, poor housing and separation from family (Jarman 1992). It is not uncommon for primary care professionals to have full responsibility for such people, who are unable to engage in secondary or specialist care. Some families are alienated by cultural or racial prejudice or have too few personal resources to seek talking therapy. Many people find referral to specialist mental health services stigmatising and would prefer to remain in primary care. There is a perception that a health problem that is contained within the community is more manageable and therefore less severe. Even when secondary services are available, there may be long waiting lists for psychotherapy or counselling, and it will be the primary care team who will have to carry the patient and partner. In response to this, a growing number of primary care practices employ their own counsellors, clinical or counselling psychologists or have depot clinics run by CPNs, or clinics run by liaison psychiatrists.

Secondary mental health care

Secondary mental health care includes community mental health teams, in-patient and out-patient local psychiatric hospital units, psychotherapy, occupational and creative arts therapy services, social services day care and residential care settings. As indicated above, patients with mental health problems who have progressed to secondary services have a higher level of need and usually carry a psychiatric diagnosis. There are exceptions; minority ethnic communities tend to have less access to talking therapy in the community, especially if they do not speak English or even standard English (Lago and Thompson 1996; d'Ardenne and Mahtani 1999). Sometimes people are given inaccurate or incomplete psychiatric diagnoses; for example, in some parts of London, there is a very high incidence of young, single African Caribbean men who are subject to compulsory hospitalisation (Littlewood and Lipsedge 1997). Patients with learning disability or long-term problems, or who are in any trouble at all with the police, may also be treated less appropriately. Some of these groups of patients are characterised by the lack of a significant person in their lives and suffer extreme social isolation. Partners of these patients who are available are in an important position, especially when decisions about future care planning have to be made. Some partners undertake the care at home; others are motivated to seek out specialist help. It can be very hard for practitioners watching well-intentioned families come close to breaking point in their efforts to 'save' their loved one from the stigma of hospital care and from their sense of guilt at 'abandoning' their partners.

Mental health care is unique in that patients can be detained and treated against their will. Where patients are likely to harm themselves, harm others or are vulnerable to harm from others, they can and will be detained and treated by secondary mental health services. Clinicians will do all they can to elicit a voluntary admission, and the partner may be involved in explaining the reason to the patient. If this cannot be achieved, the patient may be admitted involuntarily. This may leave the consenting partner, and the relationship, damaged. At its most extreme, the patient may see the partner as having betrayed trust and colluded with the clinician to achieve their incarceration. Such scars may continue long after the illness has been treated and the patient is discharged. Couples usually have access for visits to each other during hospital care. Privacy is afforded them but sexual intimacy is generally forbidden. The thinking behind this is that hospitals – even long-stay wards – are public places, where sexual activity would offend others in the vicinity. The other aspect is that patients with severe mental ill health may not be able to give consent. The whole topic of permitting sexual activity in mental health settings remains both controversial and therefore unresolved (d'Ardenne and McCann 1997). The exception to the partner having access will be where the partner is judged to contribute to the distress of the patient. Ward staff may ask an over-involved or anxious partner to reduce contact during care because of stress to both parties – a task that requires great sensitivity. A more extreme example of this would be where a partner is an assailant and the patient is admitted for additional reasons of safety. Mental health services for mothers and babies are now widely available in in-patient settings with all men denied entry to the unit.

Folie à deux (Kendell and Zeally 1992)

One intriguing aspect of couples living with 'madness' is the extent to which one party will begin to develop the same symptoms as the other. Patients who have fixed delusional beliefs, for example, and a logic to their thinking, will sometimes be able to persuade others of the rightfulness of their thinking. This is especially the case when the patient and partner are isolated and the partner is gullible. In time, the partner begins to share the delusions with the affected person. Psychiatrists call this folie a deux, although more than two parties can be involved, depending on the social and family circumstances of the patient. Once the couple is separated, the partner is open to persuasion from others and lets go of the delusions. The patient who has the true illness does not.

Tertiary mental health

Regional units offer specialist care for less common mental health problems, including eating disorders, post-traumatic stress disorders, substance abuse and severe personality disorders. They also provide secure in-patient units for forensic services, which include those for sexual offenders. Couples are seen for assessment, where available and appropriate, but again they have limited visiting access once treatment has begun. One or two specialist units in the UK are provided for couples with sexual and marital difficulties, where it is the couple who are the 'patient', even when it may have been one identified person with a problem during the referral.

Couple violence in mental health settings

Sexual and physical abuse including violence can be found in any clinical setting, since perpetrators and victims usually live together. Some victims become perpetrators; some become adult survivors. Many of these people face individual mental health difficulties, as well as challenges in their partnerships. Sexual abuse poses not only huge difficulties for the couple and their relationship, but also for the many relatives, professional staff and society at large, once it is disclosed or discovered. Balakrishna (1998) has described this as the 'ripple effect', and believes it stigmatises all the above. He reminds clinicians doing therapy with sexual abusers that they must realise that the community is their client as well. He quotes O'Connell, Leburg and Donaldson (1990): 'Because the community has a stake in the outcome, it has a legitimate right to know that evaluation and treatment are being conducted in a way that has a reasonable chance of accomplishing the primary purpose of preventing further victimization.' In this context, we see 'the community' as beginning with the patient's partner.

History-taking in mental health

Most professionals who work in mental health assess their patients and understand the importance of taking a family history, which will include a sexual and relationship history. Mental health practitioners often draw a family tree, or geneogram, which describes the patient's family of origin, current partnership(s) and the patient's own children. It is routine practice to elicit a psychosexual history from the patient, and clinicians are trained to discuss the impact of intimacy on patients' emotional wellbeing. Of particular relevance is how patients came to see themselves sexually and understand sexuality, as well as their development into active sexual relationships. In a study by One Plus One (Ayles and Reynolds 2001), CPNs reported being able routinely to address relationship issues with their patients. Their patients' relationship difficulties were revealed in reply to open questions about their wellbeing. More direct enquiries may be prompted by the behaviour or appearance of the patient. Examples of this included the patient talking only when the partner was absent, or the patient appearing to neglect his or her personal appearance.

Types of couple problem

Neurotic illnesses

It has been argued that all couple problems have a neurotic component (Freud 1900). The English literary scene seems to be littered with prime examples of lifelong disturbed partnerships affected by neurotic illness –

Leonard and Virginia Woolf, T.S. and Vivienne Eliot, Charles and Catherine Dickens and Percy and Mary Shelly, to name but a few. Neurotic problems can erode the quality of all couple relationships. The most common mental health problems are anxiety, phobias, obsessive-compulsive thoughts and behaviours, specific sexual and relationship difficulties, personality disorders and mild depression. Any of these can occur in both partners, sometimes as complementary to each other. It is not unusual for one partner to be identified as the patient, who is in fact 'carrying' the difficulties for the partnership. A good example is the severely agoraphobic wife who appears to be totally dependent on her spouse for outside errands. Despite her severe handicap, her partner appears to be only too willing to give up his whole time to her increasing demands and further dependency and incapacity. It is only when the couple unfold their story in assessment that the husband's lifelong sense of inadequacy, and maybe even his sexual difficulties, are described. His 'impotence' is mirrored by his wife's 'impotence'. Treating one person without the other here would be ineffective, as the solution they have found is an attempt to preserve the equilibrium in their marriage.

Couples with serious mental health needs

Depression and the couple

Poor partnerships can cause depression. Depression, and the stress of living with it, can undermine the foundations of a partnership. However, Roy (1987) has found that patients with endogenous and non-endogenous depression do not significantly differ in their risk of having pre- and post-morbid marital problems. Depressed spouses are objective enough to assess what is wrong with their relationship. They cite the following as problems:

- emotional distance from each other
- lack of sexual drive and specific dysfunction and orgasmic difficulties for the depressed partner
- loss of masculinity and femininity in the depressed partner
- guilt as a result of these sexual problems
- resentment at the partner's lack of tolerance and understanding of depression and its signs and symptoms
- lack of interest in depression
- loss of earnings, which affects depressed men more, who see their social role and value as breadwinner undermined.

Zeiba, Dudek and Jawor (1997) carried out a retrospective study of thirty-six depressed patients post-discharge over a twenty-four month period and found that relapse was more likely in patients who reported poor marital functioning. This was measured by marital satisfaction, sexual dysfunction and the number and duration of arguments. Their findings supported those of Brown and Harris (1978), who found that women who lacked a supportive marital relationship were three times more likely to become depressed than those who had a supportive relationship. Marital adjustment correlates with a better response to psychotherapy and prognosis with antidepressant medication. There is, however, a gender difference. Women are more sensitive to marital quality than men and are more likely to suffer from depression as a result of marital conflict. Men seem to benefit from the *mere presence* (our emphasis) of a spouse to a significantly greater extent than women (One Plus One 1998).

Psychosis and the couple

The sexual and relationship needs of people suffering from psychosis are an emerging topic of mental health care, with little in the psychiatric literature or sexual and relationship therapy work that addresses the couple within the field of psychosis. Yet the partner can do much to help understand and ameliorate the suffering of the patient and the family (McCann 1994; d'Ardenne and McCann 1997). Crowe and Ridley (1990) are couple therapists who work in a mental health setting, which includes patients with serious mental disorders. They make it clear that clinicians must 'respect the treatment being given for the psychotic condition'. Nevertheless, they would always seek problems between the couple that extend beyond the illness. Leff and Vaughan (1981) and Falloon, Boyd and McGill (1984) similarly emphasise the importance of medication to treat the psychosis and educating the relatives in the nature and progress of the illness (see below).

Education about psychosis

Families in general, and partners in particular, have been shown to benefit from relative support groups where they are given basic information about the causes, diagnosis, treatment and prognosis of the illness. The response of the partner often includes fear, panic, anger and bewilderment in the changes that occur in the person with psychosis. Here education provides a chance to normalise their experiences and understand them in a wider context. They can also put questions to mental health teams about the specific issues around their own situation, and learn about the importance of treatment compliance.

Psychoeducation

Some educational programmes entail 'psychoeducation', which aims to help relatives identify family dynamics that maintain or aggravate stress, so that they can learn ways to reduce that stress and find other ways to express and respond to need. Falloon and Liberman (1983) and Leff and Vaughan (1981) have demonstrated that the probability of relapse and the need for readmission to hospital for patients who are treated in this way by their partners and families is reduced.

The stigma of serious mental illness

Public understanding and attitudes held about people suffering from psychosis leave much to be desired. Patients suffer the primary effects of a devastating illness, which erodes the personality and interpersonal functioning, often deprives them of their education or occupation and results in severe social isolation and financial difficulty. Their greatest suffering, however, may come from the stigma and social isolation that result from the ignorance of their friends and family about the nature of the illness itself.

Many first episodes of psychosis occur when an individual is still an adolescent, and does not have a spouse or partner. In subsequent years the patient may experience unresolved symptoms or a relapse and readmission to hospital, and it is here that the partner can help the patient. Education about psychosis, and a partner willing to share with friends and relatives more information about the illness, can do much to break down prejudice and overcome fear and stigma.

Loss of social skill is a major effect of psychosis. Patients become withdrawn and internally preoccupied, and lose the capacity to be with others. They need continuous feedback, guidance and reassurance about the appropriateness of their behaviour from partners and those who care for them.

Psychosis invades all parts of the individual's thinking and feeling and often undermines self-worth and self-confidence. The patient cannot concentrate, initiate the simplest of everyday activities or hold a conversation for any length of time and is constantly distracted by internal processes, including delusions or hallucinations. A partner can remember the person as he or she was and continue to relate to and cherish the whole person. This loving care allows the patient to find self-worth and the confidence to persevere with treatment.

Some of the negative symptoms of schizophrenia include self-neglect and poor motivation to wash or attend to physical care and hygiene. A person in hospital will receive nursing care; a patient in the community will depend more on family and partner to persevere with self-care and not blame the patient for being 'dirty' or 'lazy'. These negative symptoms, part of the disease process, are perhaps some of the most difficult. They erode the affectional bonds and may incite partners' and practitioners' anger, frustration and despair (d'Ardenne and McCann 1997). At this stage the patient is very vulnerable and exquisitely sensitive to the withdrawal of others. The carer's difficulties need to be addressed urgently to prevent a major relapse.

Organic mental disorders

We include here head injuries, pre-senile dementias, brain tumours, strokes and Korsakoff's syndrome and other alcohol-related illnesses – all of which may entail not only serious physical and psychiatric symptoms, but also important personality changes and huge disruption to the relationship (Oddy 2001). Many of the issues described in the section on psychosis apply here, where it is the partner who may be the chief carer and who will be making the most substantive lifestyle adaptations. Typically, the patient will observe that the partner may look the same as before, but that the illness has changed him or her into somebody else. Their loss can be incalculable and will place the severest test on their loyalty and commitment to the relationship. Health services that are stretched will always prioritise the patient; carers are often left to fend for themselves, but may obtain help through such organisations as Headway or Al-Anon or self-help groups, see Resources List, p. 130.

Sexual problems and mental health

There is a causal and resultant link between sexual difficulty and poor mental health. Patients with anxiety, depression or obsessive-compulsive disorders often complain about sexual difficulties, and those with sexual dysfunction also complain of depression and anxiety. Couples who are referred for specific sex therapy have varied outcomes. Where one partner is in a severe anxiety state, the couple will benefit more from anxiety management prior to undertaking specific sexual therapy. Where one partner suffers obsessional traits, which directly interfere with the sexual relationship, a behavioural intervention with the couple will be initially more useful, if the symptoms are not too severe. Couples coping with mild depression or anxiety need to be considered as candidates for specific sex therapy.

A typical difficulty that depressed people have is that they have lost interest in sex, rather than that they have lost sexual performance (Beck 1967). Beaumont (1977) confirmed that the most common effect of depression in men and women is 'impaired libido'. In fact, one fifth of the subjects in Beaumont's study had discontinued sexual intercourse altogether after becoming depressed.

The role of the relationship in eating disorders is also complex and interactive. For example, women suffering anorexia nervosa have many problems with their sexuality. This eating disorder, leading to weight loss and amenorrhoea can create significant difficulties for the partner, is thought to be an avoidance of adult sexuality and often affects adolescent girls, who delay their puberty or even reverse it by extreme loss of weight (Fairburn and Cooper 1996). In such cases, it will be the patient's family of origin, and in particular her parents, rather than her partner, who are likely to be key figures in her recovery. Some young men suffer from anorexia, and although this is rare, cases are increasing.

Hawton (1985) believes that 'severe psychiatric disorder in either partner precludes immediate sex therapy'. Once again, the patient's mental distress needs to be treated prior to dealing with the couple's problems. This principle applies where either partner has serious and continuing alcohol abuse. Sex therapy in this instance should be considered only after a *reasonable* (our emphasis) period of alcohol abstinence. We would argue that 'reasonable' here means that which is agreed between the couple and the clinician prior to treatment.

At a time when sexual and marital intimacy may be at its lowest, and where the sexual and intimate needs of the partner may be quite neglected, it is paradoxical that the patient may show sexual disinhibition and become increasingly unable to keep sexual boundaries. Although this is an aspect of the mental disorder, such symptoms are understandably very distressing to the partner, and it may be important to reassure and support the partner through this. An important medication to control manic episodes, lithium carbonate, can reduce sexual appetite. But it also harms the unborn child. Couples have to face not only sexual problems, but, critically, those around effective contraception. This not only places a great burden on the couple, who have to deal with great mental distress, but also interferes with their fertility.

In schizophrenia, sexual drive is often reduced and, again, much psychiatric medication has a dampening effect on drive and performance. Patients, and still less their partners, are often not informed about this and the long-term effect it is likely to have on what may already be a stressed relationship. There is a generally held belief among clinicians that the loss of sexual drive is a regrettable but acceptable side-effect set against the even more distressing hallucinations or delusions that occur in psychosis. Whilst this may be true, there is now growing emphasis on ensuring that patient and partner understand the situation and are part of that decision.

Patients' views

Much of what has already been described earlier in the chapter refers to how clinicians can provide an opportunity for the couple to support and understand each other within the context of their own mental health. We have already raised awareness of including the partner in history-taking, education, care planning, listening, communication, readjustment and treatment compliance. Patients also have a view.

A survey by Faulkner (1997) of people experiencing mental health problems examined the strategies people used to cope with mental health problems. It was found that sufferers used a range of activities and resources to help themselves on a day-by-day basis, often in conjunction with medication. Activities ranged from psychotherapy, counselling and complementary therapies, to hobbies, leisure activities and sport. They also found that religious and spiritual beliefs were significant. We believe that partners have a primary role in sharing those initiatives and supporting the activity as much as possible. It is easier for a couple to initiate, pursue and maintain such strategies, and the sharing of them is intrinsically beneficial for the relationship. Additional bonuses include improved communication and decision-making, a sense of achievement, self-confidence and self-esteem, and a sense of fun and creativity.

Some of the above do not necessarily improve psychiatric symptoms, but they all significantly contribute to what is known as subjective quality of life (QOL). Priebe, Oliver and Kaiser (1999) have shown that people suffering serious mental illness must actively increase their QOL if they are to make other kinds of therapeutic progress. Partners and clinicians working with sufferers have a vital role to play here. The QOL domains include whether the patient has a close friend, which includes a partner, whether the patient is satisfied with family relationships, including the partner, and whether or not the patient is satisfied with his or her sex life.

What is the role of the health professional?

Users of mental health services in Faulkner's survey (1997) itemised the need for clinicians to listen. They include the following recommendations:

- Everyone in contact with mental health services has the right to have someone to talk to, the right to be listened to and to be taken seriously, particularly in times of crisis; this may not be a formal talking treatment but may be the time and space to talk with a worker, friend, or person of their choice.
- All crisis services, hospital admission wards and accident and emergency departments should make available to people the opportunity to talk to someone, or to contact the person they most want to talk to in a crisis.

Psychiatrists, general practitioners, CPNs, keyworkers and care managers provide information about self-help alternatives to service users. As we have already stressed earlier in the chapter, the partner of the mental health service user is likely to be the main provider of these opportunities. The clinician can support and educate the partner in this role and ensure that the couple are working towards the same goals as expressed above.

Case study

Susan went to see her family doctor with sleep difficulties, low back pain and minor symptoms of anxiety. Her doctor initially prescribed medication, which was of limited value, but Susan kept returning, so the doctor offered her more time to talk about life at home. She disclosed that her husband, John, was accusing her of 'frigidity'. Susan had gone to a marital counsellor to talk about 'her' problems, but had not informed or involved John at any stage.

The family doctor was able to reassure Susan that there was nothing wrong with her physically, but that she wanted to see both of them. Susan and John described many stresses in their relationship: money, teenage children and disagreements about unwillingness on her part to have sex. As John began to open up, it soon became clear to the GP that John was struggling with severe financial pressures and presented with a clinical depression. He relied on sexual intimacy to relieve symptoms of self-dislike, despair and guilt, and was angry when Susan withheld contact. She avoided sex because of the lack of reciprocal affection. The more they both spoke, the more it became clear that John was the patient and Susan the partner. He was able finally to acknowledge his depression and the need for treatment, and Susan was freed of the role she had adopted as the 'sick' partner. Once his depression improved, both partners were able to re-engage with the counsellor and deal with longstanding problems and previous betrayals that had also eroded their marriage.

Case study

James is a forty-nine-year-old Jamaican with a thirty-year history of schizophrenia. He lives with his partner of twenty-five years, Anita, and their daughter in a maisonette in East London. James is well maintained in the community and has a good relationship with a CPN, who knows the family very well. James' son has recently moved out to live with his girlfriend, and the CPN notices that James and Anita have started to argue more. She blames James for never having worked, as she has had to throughout their life together. James withdraws and stops taking his medication. The CPN becomes anxious that James is in danger of relapse and asks to see the couple together. He helps James by asking Anita to express her fears and frustrations without blame. She is able to say that she is worried about the loss of her son's companionship, support and financial contribution to the family. The CPN realises that the change in family structure has precipitated this impending crisis and he will need to educate and support James and Anita through their loss and readjustment. He suggests to Anita that she attends a local relatives' support group where she will learn more about expressed emotion and form new networks and possibly friends.

Guidelines for good practice

- In history-taking, explore sexual and relationship issues with the patient very gently. Clinicians may find such exploration difficult. An easier approach to relationship history-taking might entail saying to the patient: 'You're married, aren't you? Tell me more about yourself!' An apparently naive and open-ended question becomes an invitation to the patient to define illness within an interpersonal context.
- It is easier to be non-judgemental with a sick patient than with a spouse who seems to be aggravating a mental health problem. Use your supervisor or time with your manager to work out your assumptions and prejudices about your patient's partner.
- Try to avoid collusion with the partner of a mental health patient. Partners are often isolated individuals who pull health professionals to them as they see their burden increasing. Avoid secrets; encourage the partner to find a way of sharing with the patient. If you become aware of collusion, or even attraction, share this with your supervisor and try to work out what is happening.
- Taking psychotropic medication is a key factor in reducing symptoms, improving quality of life and reducing risk. Clinicians can listen to couples who complain about unpleasant side-effects and help them understand the risks of non-compliance. Explain as fully as possible the importance of medication compliance, both with the patient and partner together, and if necessary, separately. Help the partner generate ideas for making medication compliance easier. For example, can it be a shared responsibility? Can tablet-taking be attached to some ritual in home life to ensure it is reliably and regularly taken? Can the partner encourage the patient to persevere with medicine even when there are no symptoms? Can the partner watch carefully for small changes in mental state and come back to you quickly if they occur?
- Explain the effects of medication on sex drive, or encourage the couple to ask the psychiatrist who prescribes it to explain. Couples who

experience loss of libido because of medication can be encouraged to share this and find other ways of being intimate.

- Encourage the partner to attend carers' groups. These provide information about mental illness, reduce stigma, normalise a caregiver's daily experiences and encourage families to be more tolerant and positive in their attitudes. Most of all, they provide vital networks and social support to families who become increasingly isolated by having to deal with the effects of mental illness.
- Ask the partner to describe and remember the patient as they were and continue to relate to and cherish the whole person. This loving care allows the patient to find self-worth and the confidence to persevere with treatment.
- Health professionals can educate the partner to offer a structured self-care programme, which will include gentle prompting, modelling and encouragement. Feedback and affection will allow the patient to establish a structured routine and will ensure that the partner does not become physically repelled by neglected hygiene. Perseverance and consistency produces surprisingly good results.
- Explain to the partner the importance of both of them maintaining social contact with friends and family. Ask the partner to encourage visitors at home and hospital, even when the sufferer seems most inaccessible. You can encourage the partner to explain the need for brief and frequent contact and a very gradual resumption of friendship on a graded and structured basis.
- Ensure that partners have access to family therapy where this is indicated and offered, and reassure them of the importance of taking a low-key attitude to the psychotic family member, by not being too critical or controlling.
- If your patient has a partner, are they always invited to care planning meetings and discharge meetings?

CHAPTER 8

Chronic Illness – sharing the load

Introduction

The word 'chronic' signifies a long-term medical condition; that means a course that can be stable, unpredictable or progressive. The word comes from the Greek chronos, meaning 'time'. Well-known examples include arthritis, cancer, diabetes, heart disease, multiple sclerosis and stroke. Chronic illnesses are health problems that typically result in challenges to physical and psychosocial functioning, to the performance of social roles at work and leisure, and in the family and friendships. It is hard to think of any long-term condition, therefore, that does not have implications for the relationship of the patient with the partner or for sexual activity within that relationship. This chapter considers some conditions in detail, but also describes notable similarities in the effects of a wide range of chronic medical problems on relationships that patients have with their families, and in particular, their partners.

Over the last hundred years, the principal cause of death has shifted from infectious diseases, especially respiratory disease, to chronic illness – in particular cardiovascular diseases and cancer (Social Trends 2000). People may be living longer, but they and their partners will also be carrying the burden of chronic health problems and physical disability for longer.

Interest in the effects of chronic illness on personal relationships has come from three sources: personal relationship research, research on social support and coping research. Research in these areas has been more concerned with the impact of various stressors on physical and mental ill health, and less on what actually happens between couples as they attempt to cope with illness (Cutrona 1996). However, relationship research has increased our understanding of how life events such as illness affect close relationships (Lyons and Meade 1995).

Rationale

Not all chronic diseases are easy to diagnose, nor do they follow a predictable path. The unpredictability of the course of multiple sclerosis, for example, is particularly disruptive to intimate relationships and sexuality (Brooks and Matson 1982). Issues that were cited by the women in this study included: dealing with the symptoms in the relationship; finding a shared meaning with their partner; dealing with the gap between what is, and what ought to be (Calmen 1984); and normalising the social role (Rusbult and Buunk 1993). Women in particular suffered from the desire to be the perfect wife, mother, housewife and friend, and at the same time as coping with a chronic illness or a sick partner, as well as the need to be a patient or partner with chronic illness in a clinical setting.

The patient who may be coping with physical disability, pain, exhaustion or emotional turmoil is placed in a position of increasing dependence on a carer. However good professional care is in the community, most patients with chronic ill health will be cared for by a relative, typically their partner. Nobody wants to be a burden to any partner, but there is plenty of evidence to show that the 'burden' of care inevitably falls on that person, whose own needs may be neglected both by self, the patient, the family and the wider community. The nature of marriage is intimate, and assumptions are made by all about 'in sickness and in health'. This implies that a carer, who also happens to be a spouse, 'should not complain'. What is more, the carer may feel that the support previously available within the relationship can no longer be accessed. The partner has become a patient, and any sense of burden about the illness cannot be shared with the patient. The rationale of this chapter is to make the clinician aware of the changes that occur in the relationship in step with the illness, and to help the partner in his or her role as the primary source of support for the patient.

This chapter is also intended to help the reader see chronic illness as experienced by the couple, rather than as an individual problem in a patient who happens to live with a partner. We know that many chronic illnesses are more likely to affect couples in later life, and indeed, illnesses such as dementia, coronary heart disease and stroke will merit more detailed consideration in the next chapter. Chronic ill health may also be the consequence of injury; we have described this in Chapter 6, 'Trauma'. This chapter does not concern itself with children's long-term illness – this is covered in part in Chapter 5, 'Sick Children', although we recognise that there are many features common to both healthcare topics.

We have not been able to cover all chronic illnesses, but we shall describe many of the clinical settings in which they occur, as well as problems common to couples. We have a special section on sexuality, as this is an area that has been described as difficult for clinicians, patients and their partners.

Clinical settings

Chronic illness is widespread in health settings and affects all walks of life. Clinicians are most likely to meet their chronically ill patient in out-patient, community or home settings. Primary care professionals will be likely to retain much responsibility for ongoing care once a patient is discharged from hospital, and it is in primary care that the treatment plan is implemented. The patient's partner will be a key element in the care plan, and unless clinicians can collaborate with the partner, rehabilitation or ongoing care may be jeopardised.

At home, once the diagnosis has been understood, the vision of the future changes for both patient and partner. Few couples will have anticipated such a drastic change in their status. Long-term illness threatens the health and longevity of the patient. It also affects the wellbeing of the patients' partners, their social identity, performance in their respective roles, financial security and long-term plans. Chronic illness changes not only how the couple see each other, but also how they see their world and how they are perceived socially. Affected couples may not be initially aware of how quickly their social networks will drop away. They are managing pain, fatigue, immobility and treatment – all likely to reduce their social networks. The illness dominates the landscape and may well limit social and sports contact, or even lead to the termination of work. Relationships with others are also impoverished, leading to poor companionship for both patient and partner. It is rare for couples to reverse that trend without the proactive support of self-help groups or informed clinicians.

After a diagnosis has been given, couples face their new status and adopt a number of strategies, sometimes in contradictory fashion. Those who are in denial will proceed as if nothing has changed and wait until an accident or critical event forces them into disclosure, perhaps in an uncontrolled way. Couples who share a diagnosis with others may have to face ignorance and prejudice. Consider the response of some communities to patients with HIV or the hurdles faced by patients suffering epilepsy, schizophrenia or malignant disease.

Couples who are already struggling to maintain their relationship may find that they lack the resources to deal with the added complexities of illness. The partner can become overwhelmed by the immediate demands of taking over the ill person's household responsibilities, compensating for lost income, driving to treatments, watching suffering, facing the fear of loss and coping with the partner's emotional reactions. The regular rhythm of interaction and support is broken, causing new tensions and great physical and emotional upheaval for them both. Not only do they both have to manage their own stress, they must respond to and cope with the distress of the other. In fact, spouses are as much at risk of psychological distress as the patient with chronic illness (Coyne, Ellard and Smith 1990). For a relationship to survive, couples must find ways of addressing any imbalance in support.

Medical settings

Hospitalisation occurs during crises, relapse, for ongoing treatment or for respite care for patients and their partners. There are important issues for the clinician and the couple to be negotiated about the treatment setting, such as the timing of a respite bed.

There remain other physical, organisational and therapeutic barriers to the chronically ill or disabled patient and partner. Health gains or even health maintenance are best achieved if the health settings are appropriate, provide good access, good communication, adequate support, mobility and transport, space, parking and a sensitivity and understanding about the stigma of an illness. Such requirements are desirable for patients with long-term needs who will be using a health service perhaps for the rest of their lives. But it also raises more interesting ideas about where clinical settings exist.

Chronic illness requires social rehabilitation as well as a medical input. The workplace, the school or the local sports centre may be just as significant for health decisions and care as a more traditional clinic in a district general hospital. For example, a chronically obese patient may benefit more from a prescription for aerobic exercise planned and organised by the staff of the local sports centre than attendance at a hospital obesity clinic. The patient may find this less stigmatic and will be able to share the visit with a partner or friend.

The methods that partners use to manage the stress of chronic illness change over time in response to the health challenges. For example, when the main car driver in the relationship is no longer able to drive, the partner will have to undertake all activities that depend on the car – shopping, the school run, holidays, visiting and healthcare. Gradually, the partner may have to start to accommodate a patient who is slow or using a stick. Then the carer will need to learn to dismantle and take a wheelchair in uncomfortable or even risky circumstances. Later still, the carer will need to plan journeys with the use of disability transport or ambulances, and timetable trips accordingly.

Couple problems

We have already described the profound challenge to relationships posed by chronic illness. Changes in the relationship are extensive and can include emotional and psychosexual difficulties.

Psychological issues

Chronic illness creates substantial psychological distress. The highest risk factors in suicide are: being male, over 65 years, single and chronically ill or disabled (Social Trends 2000). All patients with chronic ill health suffer a loss and can expect the emotions comparable to a bereavement. Depression is almost to be expected. Depression is a significant stressor for both patient and well partner and adds to the perceived degree of disability that they are sharing and responding to. Depression in either party is highly stressful and likely to be a cause of emotional distress and/or guilt in the other. Seigal (1997) defines grief as the giving up of some past reality, which may include ordinary hopes and expectations for the future. Couples who are facing the loss together need to face loss explicitly, as long-term avoidance causes further emotional and social problems for them.

One of these is anger. Anger can also exacerbate the illness process. In a study of the effects of anger on chronic illness, over 30 per cent of partners caring for arthritic patients named their partner's negative mood, namely anger, as one of their major stresses in daily life (Revenson and Majerovitz 1991). In chronic obstructive pulmonary disease the severity of symptoms is a significant predictor of how angry patients are. Patients become angrier as they face illness-related losses and the accompanying decline of function. Their spouses report that patient irritability is a major source of stress in their role as carer.

Anger is also related to the extent to which the partner who provides care perceives care-giving as a burden. The perception is not related to the objective amount of work or to the severity or longevity of the symptoms. It is related to their quality of life, overall level of emotional distress, loneliness, amount of other informal care providers and unmet demand for the psychosocial care of the patient (Scholte op Reimer et al. 1998). Scholte op Reimer et al.'s study was based on stroke victims, but similar patterns have been found with the partners of dementia patients, and have significant implications for healthcare professionals supporting the patient and partner.

Some resentful caregivers are overprotective (intrusive and controlling) and may overestimate the amount of support they actually provide to their sick partner (Stephens and Clark 1997). There is even some evidence that 'support' can interfere with the extent to which patients regain strength and functioning.

Perhaps a sadder aspect of their disposition is that angry carers may alienate other support givers and create further isolation of the couple.

Not all expressed emotion between couples with chronic disease is negative. Scholte op Reimer et al. (1998) found that partners who cared for stroke victims and perceived them as a burden nevertheless reported an increase in pride, gratification and a feeling of closeness to their sick partner, especially as the illness progressed and the disability increased.

Acceptance of illness or disablity is an extension of the grieving process and entails insight into what has been lost and a capacity to gain a realistic picture of what the present and future condition of the patient is likely to be. Some patients see acceptance as 'giving up the battle'. Partners can help them if a conversation can be had about what has been lost and what can actually be fought for. Seigal (1997) estimates that on average patients with chronic disability take up to two years to accept their loss, which means that they may be two years mentally out of date with their actual physical condition.

Another issue for couples sharing long-term illness is loss of social and psychological role. Carers perceive their partners as already burdened, and feel they should therefore not have any other distress to face. They may be anxious that a sick partner should not be made angry or worried, and undermine the patient's capacity to assume normal family relationships. Conflict that is avoided becomes conflict that is unresolved, and the partnership is undermined as a resource for both parties.

People with long-term illness suffer the stigma placed on them by society, and the resultant lowered self-esteem and even self-blame that attach to the sufferer. Consider the terms 'epileptic', 'diabetic', 'schizophrenic' and ' spastic', all used until very recently. It is easy to see why people see themselves as *being* the illness they bear, rather than individuals who have many roles, and who also happen to be *suffering* from an illness. Partners relate to patients outside their sickness and have many opportunities to normalise that experience and help neighbours and friends to see the person and not the illness.

Sexual intimacy

An extension of stigma is the experience people with long-term illness have of being asexual or having few sexual needs. This perception is held by many caring for those with illness and by sufferers themselves. Seigal (1997) has described how carers often find they cannot combine the roles of sexual partner and nurse, and that this needs to be taken into account when deciding who takes care of the partner's bodily needs. Bancroft (1989) shows how the effects of long-term illness can affect sexual relationships in three major domains, and how these have historically been overlooked by medical staff in their long-term management of illness.

First of these are the specific physical effects of a chronic condition, for example, vascular changes or neurological degeneration which can literally prevent sexual activity or seriously limit its frequency or intensity. Non-specifically, pain, tiredness, lack of desire or spasticity can make the expression of physical affection and sexual activity difficult or even impossible.

Second, the psychological effects of chronic illness affect the individual by way of embarrassment, feeling sexually unattractive or simply feeling of less value because of the condition. The impact on the partnership can take many forms. The partner may feel guilty for even thinking about sex when the patient has faced life-threatening illness or disability. The partner may make incorrect assumptions about the partner's desire for sex or the impact of sexual activity on the course of the illness. The relationship may have shifted when the partner became a carer to that of parent, when the sexual dynamic has also shifted and become less appropriate. The partner can also start to see the patient as less attractive, or begin to see the self as less attractive by virtue of association. Lastly, the partner may have concern or even fear of sexual activity in conditions such as severe hypertension or ischaemic heart disease, and refuse even to discuss the matter with the patient or health professional.

Third, treatment affects the ways couples see themselves and their sexual intimacy. Surgery, and subsequent disfigurement, radiotherapy, drugs, restrictions in diet, changes in behaviour including smoking, drugs and alcohol intake, will impact not only on the patient, but also on the partner.

Intimacy occurs at many levels in a relationship, and sexual intimacy is profoundly affected by chronic disease. The effects are at a physical as well as a psychological level. For example, a patient on renal dialysis will suffer fatigue and low libido (Bancroft 1989). Other chronic illnesses (arthritis, rheumatism, coronary disease, stroke, diabetes, cancer and TB) all impact not just on patients and their sense of themselves as sexually attractive people, but also, as we have pointed out in the introduction, on the way they are perceived by their partners.

Patients with chronic disease may lose their sexual identity. The well-intentioned trend in hospital to provide mixed sex wards can, paradoxically, aggravate this loss. The patient role is an individual and asexual one. Health professionals still have difficulty recognising their patients with chronic illnesses as sexual beings with sexual needs. Practitioners have described problems in initiating discussions about sexuality, responding to the topic if it is raised by the patient or partner, picking up on cues and providing permission for sex to be discussed as a legitimate personal need.

Specific chronic complaints

Diabetes

Diabetes is an endocrine disorder arising from an inadequate supply of insulin. It produces a wide range of metabolic and degenerative effects, which are not fully understood. Because diabetes tends to damage peripheral and autonomic nerves, it causes degeneration in small blood vessels throughout the body and interferes with vision, circulation to the lower limbs and, of course, with sexual function.

It has been recognised for over two centuries that diabetes directly affects the erectile function of men, but there is now recognition that the picture is complex, multifactorial and involves psychological and social as well as organic factors. Older men with diabetes who had longer duration of the illness, poor glycaemic control, alcohol intake, neuropathy and retinopathy were also more likely to have erection difficulties. Their over-all quality of life was also less satisfactory and they experienced greater levels of anxiety or distress and lower levels of sexual interest (McCulloch et al. 1984).

Female patients with diabetes present an even more complex picture. First, younger patients with Type 1 (insulin-dependent) diabetes are more likely to have been diagnosed before choosing a life partner and tend then to select more supportive and accepting partners. They then face the physical challenges of poorer reproductive and obstetric health within that relationship, and are no different from controls in terms of sexual desire or sexual function. Women with Type 2 (non-insulin-dependent) diabetes have to make decisions later in their lives with their existing part-ners, who may or may not be willing or understanding. These women rate themselves as sexually less attractive, less happy and satisfied with their partners, and less happy with sexuality in general. Since these women are less ill than the Type 1 population, it might be reasonable to conclude that psychogenic factors are every bit as important, if not more so, than organic factors in the cause of poor sexual relationships in women with diabetes (Harland and Huws 1997).

Cardiovascular disease

Studies of men and women following coronary bypass surgery have shown that both report a deterioration of their relationships in the area of sexuality; in men it is sexual arousal; in women it is sexual desire. After myocardial infarction, both sexes express fear of intercourse or orgasm as a precipitant of a further attack, or even death. Both sexes and their part-ners are reluctant to raise the issue after an attack, but both respond to appropriate counselling and the provision of information from health pro-fessionals. Men and women with cardiovascular disease and hypertension report less satisfactory relationships than healthy controls, but this differ-ence is not significant if they are matched with controls who have other chronic disease. Many couples describe a vicious circle thus: they have a stressful relationship and do not communicate or share physical intimacy. They indulge in eating or drinking alcohol or smoking to reduce stress, which aggravates their physical symptoms. This causes further stress and a further deterioration of their relationship. Their symptoms make them fearful of even thinking about sex, let alone discussing it with their partners, who are equally frightened of 'killing them off'.

Chronic renal failure

Men and women who have chronic renal failure have a high rate of sexual dysfunction and a marked reduction of sexual interest (Nichols 1991). In addition, they will experience the disruption of two hospital visits a week of eight hours' duration. The treatment involves painful and uncomfortable procedures, which can make patients feel like laboratory animals and less like sexual people. Many sufferers of renal failure have described dialysis as a 'living death' and the depression that accompanies this experience contaminates the relationship and reduces the desire for sex.

Haemodialysis patients have less happy relationships with their partners than transplant patients, as well as poorer sexual function, although it is difficult to ascertain which is cause and which is effect. Home dialysis places exceptional strain on the partner and on the relationship in general. The patient may suffer general malaise, infertility, substantial dietary restrictions and some social exclusion, to say nothing of uncertain life expectancy. Renal transplant patients fare much better, in terms of their symptoms as well as their expressed satisfaction with their relationships with their partners.

Cerebrovascular disease

There is evidence that, after a stroke, couples who can reciprocally support each other cope better in their relationships than those where there is emotional support only from the care-giving partner (Stephens and Clark 1997). Similarly, rehabilitation is less successful if the carer (usually the partner) is stressed or depressed (Scholte op Reimer et al. 1998). Hawton (1984) found that where couples had been sexually active prior to the stroke, partners responded better to psychosexual counselling than those who had not been active. With male patients, an interest in sexual activity returned within seven weeks of the initial stroke.

Brain damage

A study carried out in Israel (Kravetz et al. 1995) looked at 36 couples where the man had long-standing brain damage and found that this negatively affected both partners' self-concept. Both partners in the brain-damaged group suffered an increase in conflict and marital dysfunction, some of which was directly attributable to the men's neurological symptoms. The men did not perceive the marriage as being more vulnerable than a control group of non-disabled married men. Their wives, however, did differ from the controls in as much as they saw their marriage as more vulnerable than before. What makes this study interesting is that chronic disease can impact more negatively on the spouse than on the victim. Health professionals need to show particular sensitivity to the support needs of the partner who also may have changed as a result of the disease.

Spinal injuries

There are more survivors of wars and road traffic accidents than ever who, sadly, have life-long spinal injuries. These have a devastating effect on the patients and their partners. Most spinal injury patients are young males and experience no change in their sexual desire or desire to give pleasure to a partner, who may also be the primary caregiver. Clinicians have an interest in the effect of spinal injury on sexual function and, in particular, the difference between men and women. Psychological factors are a significant feature; male patients suffer more in terms of loss of sexual function and associated loss of self-esteem and confidence. Kolodny, Masters and Johnson (1979) suggest that couples do benefit from counselling and support, but that the reasons why and how this helps remain unclear.

Multiple sclerosis

Demyelination of the nerves means that victims of MS experience chronic fatigue, loss of sensory and motor function, and an uncertain prognosis for an untreatable disease. The disease leads to specific loss of sexual function and also affects sufferers' libido and self-esteem. The unpredictability of symptoms and periods of remission mean that patients and partners have constantly to change their strategy in response to the illness and their expectations of quality of life. The relationship, like the illness, becomes a roller coaster of hope and despair.

Ostomies

Chronic illnesses of the bowel, including inflammatory disease (of younger) and malignant disease (of older) patients, can be treated by surgically opening the bowel in the abdominal wall. Whilst this treatment may be life-saving, the presence of a bag of liquid faeces on the abodominal wall, the loss of sensation in the pelvic area and the constant fear of odour or leakage represent a sexual challenge for the patient and partner, and leave couples facing chronic difficulties in how to express and enjoy physical intimacy. There is evidence that patients and partners do find this psychologically stressful, and it leads to significant depression and anxiety (Huish, Kumar and Stones 1998).

Malignancy and sexual identity

All surgery leaves scars – whether physical, psychological or emotional. Patients who have had extensive procedures, such as hysterectomies, mastectomies or prostatectomies, have to adjust in long-term relationships to a change in their perception of their mortality, themselves and their sexual identity (Weijmar Schultz et al. 1992). Patients and partners have to deal with life-long medication regimes, fear, uncertainty, mutilation and changes.

In conclusion, there appears to be a recognisable difference in sexual difficulties between the sexes in chronic disease. Men typically complain of loss of performance, whilst still experiencing the same drive and interest. The loss affects their self-esteem and they avoid affection in case it leads to an expectation to perform. Their partners are thus deprived of both sexual intimacy and affection. On the other hand, women more often complain that chronic illness interferes with their interest in sex and sexual arousal. They have fewer performance difficulties, but do suffer from a sense of being less attractive.

Case study

Pauline and Phil have lived together for nearly thirty years, of which sixteen have been spent coping with Phil's multiple sclerosis. His illness has progressed to a point when he can no longer hold down his teaching job and, although he is adequately insured, Phil finds the loss of his profession particularly painful. For the first time since diagnosis, he sees himself as an MS sufferer rather than as a teacher who happens to have MS. He deteriorates physically, but also becomes clinically depressed and stops attending your physiotherapy outpatient clinic for therapy he badly needs.

Pauline arrives in the clinic in tears and explains what has happened and why Phil no longer wishes to attend. Having listened to Pauline and asked her about her deeper fears, you agree to call Phil at home. When you telephone him, Phil seems vague and denies that there are any difficulties. He says that there is no longer any point in trying to keep up a therapy regime when the illness is eventually going to kill him, and asks to be discharged from your clinic. Pauline is distraught and asks for a joint appointment.

When you see them, it is clear that Phil has lost weight and has substantial sleep difficulties. His mood is rather flat, and although he has seen his GP recently, you remain unconvinced about how much his mental state has been assessed and treated. You ask them if they will allow you to write to their family doctor and request a referral to the local community mental health team for an initial assessment. You strongly recommend that Pauline asks for a carer's assessment, and that she be invited to as many interviews as Phil is willing to have with her. Since Pauline is the main driver for the couple, Phil is quite dependent on her and agrees to allow her to attend. You set up a follow-up appointment in a couple of months' time to establish how much progress has been made.

Case study

You are a local GP who runs a well women clinic. Two of your patients, Kate and Jenny, are a couple who have set up home in the last five years. Kate has a diagnosis of hypertension, but has continued to smoke and has a significant weight problem. Kate has received plenty of health education, but remains resolute in pursuing her chosen lifestyle. For years she was in an unhappy and abusive marriage in which food and cigarettes were perhaps one of her few comforts. Now, she resents being 'told what to do' and Kate and Jenny have started to have substantial arguments about what Jenny perceives as Kate's risky behaviour.

Jenny is ten years older than Kate. Her former husband also smoked heavily and eventually died of lung carcinoma. She has always known about Kate's health, but believed at the start of their relationship that she would be able to save her from herself. Neither party is willing to change her position and the whole relationship is beginning to show strain.

Kate arrives in the clinic and asks you to ask Jenny to stop nagging her. You respond by giving each of them a chance to explain what she sees as the problem. As you listen, you realise that they have never really talked to each other about how Kate's high blood pressure frightens them, and how her chronic problem reflects unresolved issues in this couple's previous relationships. It is only when each has had a chance to hear the other in your presence that they begin to figure out other ways of supporting each other, without trying to control or abuse the other's freedom. They also have an opportunity to talk about how a heart attack might occur and, better still, how it might be prevented. As they leave the clinic, you hear them begin to plan to join some friends who regularly walk for exercise.

Guidelines for good practice

Clinicians may find it useful to consider the stages a couple will face in chronic illness. Initially, there will be a period of education and understanding, followed by help from the clinician to appraise the stressors implicit in their new situation. The next stage will involve the identification of adaptive tasks (what needs doing) and coping resources (restraints and opportunities) and finally working out coping strategies.

- Encourage open communication between the couple to identify and share problems, fears and frustrations. Open communication seems to be a critical component in maintaining a high-quality relationship in the context of a chronic illness.
- Clarify the emotional, sexual and practical needs of the couple by active listening.
- Offer specific disease-related information and instructions – diet, exercise, lifestyle changes – to both partners working as a health alliance.
- Foster reinforcements from outside the couple – encourage them to seek respite, a sympathetic ear. Locate and suggest the couple contact support groups as appropriate. Support groups for specific diseases now run educational programmes where both partners are encouraged to participate and learn about not only the disease, but also the effects of the disease on their relationship. Remember self-help groups do not suit every patient.
- Work with the couple to maintain equity. Suggest that the patient can find a new role by providing emotional support to the well partner. Stephens and Clark (1997) suggest that the key element of successful support is a degree of exchange and reciprocity between the couple. Negative emotions can be exchanged for positive ones provided the carer is not left bearing the brunt of the emotional burden.
- Where there are strong negative attributions – blaming and hostility – consider referring for couple therapy.
- Encourage the couple to gain strength by working as a team. Establish with them whether the patient is able to take on chores, however small. Facing seemingly overwhelming problems together can lead to mobilisation of support for one another.
- Encourage the carer and sufferer to 'reframe' caring as commitment and love, increasing self-esteem and reducing burden. Teach the couple to blame the illness for negative emotions such as anger or guilt and attribute loving kindness to the partner.
- Discuss the dangers of reinforcing pain behaviour in the affected partner and encourage words, activities and beliefs that foster recovery. Help the couple to respond with attention to each other outside the illness. Their interaction should neither reinforce helplessness nor ignore the need for nurturing and understanding.
- Reinforce the value of maintaining and developing social contacts and social role, before isolation and avoidance become a feature of the partnership.

In conclusion, we recognise that clinicians who work with couples in chronic illness face complexity. They have to work with and support the partner, since, as we have emphasised throughout this chapter, change in one will affect the other. Spouses may even suffer more from the illness than the patient. Kravetz et al. (1995), for example, show that the care-giving partner may even experience a higher level of emotional distress than the sufferer.

CHAPTER 9

Later Life – till death us do part

Introduction

The population of older adults is increasing in most parts of the Western world. In the UK, nearly half of the population will be 50 or over by 2010 (Phanjoo 2002). Definitions and perceptions of old age must, of course, reflect an ever-changing landscape. Ageism still pervades our culture, and negative stereotypes about growing old are often based on misconceptions about age and deny the individual's own experience of age within the context of culture and family life. This is especially the case in the field of intimate relationships; some of our most negative attitudes are around the idea of older couples having any kind of sexual relationship at all.

In the UK, 65-year-old men and women are both in receipt of a state pension and come under elderly health services within the National Health Service. Therefore, for the purposes of this chapter, couples over the age of 65 are our focus. We also recognise that there are enormous individual differences in ageing and that the older population ages at different rates. We recognise, for example, that many 65-year-olds are very young indeed. What is more, there is now a 'super-young' phenomenon of people who have been studied by neuropsychologists; people who look, act and feel decades younger than their chronological age, and who lead much healthier lifestyles than many others much younger than themselves (Weeks and James 1998).

Married life is likely to last longer than in previous generations for couples remaining in intact marriages. But a high divorce and remarriage rate also means that many couples are experiencing the early years of marriage in older age (Bridgewood et al. 2000). Our definition of later life marriage, therefore, includes couples who have been married a long time, older couples in a newer relationship and couples reaching grandparenthood, empty nest syndrome and retirement. In 1997, life expectancy in the UK was 74.6 years for men and 79.6 years for women (Goddard and Savage 1994). Couples, therefore, may have two decades of life together in old age before one of them dies. The proportion of older couples living together in the population is also on the increase. Forty-eight per cent of people in Great Britain over pensionable age who live in their own homes, live with their partner. The ageing of the population is leading us to a new phenomenon – an increase in the number of very long-term couples, some reaching six or even seven decades of conjugal life. This chapter explores the impact of old age and dying on the couple, as well as the buffering effect of a committed relationship on people in later life.

Rationale

It may by now be evident that many of the topics that are covered in the previous chapter on chronic ill health also feature in the lives of the elderly. Long-term health problems and old age are not, of course, the same thing. Indeed, what exactly constitutes normal ageing and what constitutes disease are hotly debated. Clearly, older people do experience an increase in healthcare needs, but that does not make their quality of life any poorer. Marriage, or at least a committed relationship, offsets in good part the ravages of illness and time. Older patients lower their expectations and are able to derive much satisfaction from their next of kin once their occupational and childrearing roles have diminished. This is in part because such activities can be a major source of stress.

Ill health

An increasing number of elderly people live many years after retirement, but inevitably health changes with age. The picture is compounded by the loss of social and occupational role, social isolation and economic poverty. Added problems include loss of mobility, over-consumption of medication, the effects of loss and bereavement, anxiety and depression. The individual needs of elderly people may impose considerable demands on the couple and their immediate families. Elderly people can be described as relatively heavy consumers of health services. People aged over 65 account for just under half of all NHS hospital and community health services use and expenditure (Social Trends 1999). Those in a higher age group are more likely to be visited by a GP at home and just over half of all prescriptions go to pensioners (Bridgewood et al. 2000). Specific illnesses that significantly affect older populations include depression, dementia, cancer, coronary disease and stroke.

The benefits of marriage in old age

Trudel, Turgeon and Piche (2000) reviewed the literature on retirement and found a varied picture. Retirement as a process is a stressful transition period, which affects couples in different ways, and reflects to some extent the capacities they have shown in earlier stages of the lifecycle to adapt to change.One thing that has clearly emerged from the literature is that the conjugal satisfaction of older people is positively associated not only with subjective quality of life measures, but also with physical and mental health (Atchley and Miller 1983). Levenson, Carstenson and Gottman (1993) investigated the relationship between health behaviours, marital status and gender in elderly people and found that marriage has positive effects on health behaviour in elderly people and, when these differ by gender, they tend to be greater for men than women. Men who become widowed or divorced may lose more than a spouse: they are also likely to give up a range of health habits that help protect against disease and early death.

Schone and Weinick (1998) also showed that marriage encourages certain healthy behaviours in younger people and demonstrated that benefits continue to later life. These behaviours included sharing, communicating on a continuous basis, caring for each other's physical and emotional needs and socialising. By contrast, those older people who were widowed or separated had fewer social outlets, and even less opportunity to develop such skills on an everyday basis.

Research (Trudel, Turgeon and Piche 2000) has shown that couples who had pre-morbid satisfactory relationships are more likely to be able to face illness or injury together and share the burden that the illness places on their everyday living. The clinician is faced with an interesting paradox with couples: one or both may be facing serious health challenges, but at the same time be enjoying a subjectively higher quality of life than in previous decades.

Levenson, Carstenson and Gottman (1993) researched the sources of pleasure in 60–70-year-old couples, and found an encouraging picture. Couples retained their interest not only in shared activities and family, but also in holidays, other people, political and current events, and plans for the future.

Clinical settings

There are specialised services in the UK for the over 65s, but equally, there are many health services that do not have an upper age limit and therefore include elders with the rest of their adult populations. The older couple may therefore present in general medical or surgical settings, accident and emergency services, diabetes, coronary care or stroke units, and of course the full range of paramedical out-patient and in-patient services. The debate continues about the advantages of inclusion or exclusion of elders in therapy settings, but it is clear that as couples live and work for longer, that greater flexibility and variety of services need to be made available to the couple. Partners in their sixties are unlikely to have the same health requirements thirty years later if they are still together.

Home is where the majority of couples in their 60s and over are likely to be seen when receiving healthcare. It is also where health professionals have a unique opportunity to experience the quality of the couple's relationship and the stresses imposed by disease process and ageing. Community care reforms in place in the UK since 1993 mean that social care, in the form of home help, meals services and day care, are provided as an alternative to residential care, and have had a significant and positive effect on the health of older people. Those living alone are more than twice as likely as couples to need social help, and 9 per cent of elders living alone will be visited by a district nurse, compared to only 3 per cent of those living with a spouse (Social Trends 1999). Local health services are organised geographically, with the family doctor as the entry point by which all other services are accessed. Older people are being discharged earlier from hospital and convalescing at home. Older people facing terminal illness are expressing a wish to be supported in their own homes until death. The expansion of the Macmillan Nursing Service is a good example of cancer care that facilitates this choice.

Among those over 65, the highest proportion of carers at home are married or cohabiting women, and older carers carry some of the heaviest burdens of care. Nearly half of those at home spend fifty or more hours a week caring for their sick partner – more than the average working hours of employees. Levenson, Carstenson and Gottman (1993) suggest that older men and women respond to the demands of their care-giving role differently. Both sexes try to deal positively with the demands of caring at home; men, however, see the role as a meaningful retirement activity – a job – and appear to derive positive feelings from 'being in charge'.

The wider community

In some areas, primary care services now have an extended range of community services targeting the needs of the over-sixties. These services are local and close to public transport, and are intended to maintain older people out of hospital care. Such facilities not only help the patient, but also provide for the carer, usually the patient's partner. Many centres have their own pharmacies, and patients are encouraged to attend clinics for regular monitoring and treatment compliance as well as for health education and heath promotion. These services are models of good practice, providing for the holistic needs of the patient and partner.

Hospital, residential and respite care

The needs of the couple may be overlooked when one is admitted to hospital or a residential setting. Each may experience the distress of separation and the loss of day-to-day contact, sharing, caring, communication and socialisation. The partner who is at home may have a sense of failure in not providing adequate practical care and support. There may also be anxieties about the quality of care for the sick partner and the difficulties – physical, financial and psychological – of gaining access as a visitor. Equally, the sick partner may share anxieties about their elderly partner coping alone.

Typically, health services and carers in residential and nursing homes overlook the intimacy needs of older couples. Younger people, including health professionals, may believe that the over-fifties no longer have sexual contact, or that if they do, it is inappropriate or even disgusting (Weeks 2002). In good palliative care, provision is made for couples' sexual privacy – whether sharing a bed or private room. Oliviere, Hargreaves and Monroe (1998) discuss gender and sexuality in their book on palliative care. Removing sex from the agenda can isolate terminally ill people even further from much needed love and acceptance. They may also be facing loss in so many areas – vitality, bodily control, faith and self confidence, control over their own destiny, energy. This principle holds true for all couples separated by health need, and it affects young and old alike.

Social and cultural settings

The needs and vulnerability of the elderly couple are connected to their increasing social isolation from the world of work and family, and increasing introspection. Some older couples may be 'turned in', and less in touch with social networks. They will need encouragement to keep in touch with life outside home and personal concerns. Older people, especially those in their ninth and tenth decades, can be more accepting, less assertive and less articulate in medical settings. There is evidence (Social Trends 1999) that the over-fifties express greater satisfaction with every aspect of service they receive from the National Health Service than those aged under fifty. They 'don't like to bother' and trust that medics will get it right. They may, therefore, need an advocate to articulate their needs and wishes. Health workers are in a unique position to provide this and demonstrate that there are people who will really listen. Some couples may have longstanding learning difficulties, or be illiterate and unable to fill in forms for financial help. They may require extra help in accessing social services and the help for them available through voluntary organisations may be spread too thinly. Income tends to fall with age, more so for women than for men. Occupational pensions for all women and minority ethnic patients are smaller than for white men (Social Trends 1999). If a spouse dies, the impact on the survivor's income is significant and again affects women more than men. In brief, financial hardship is a distinct feature of the older couple's health problems.

Couple problems

If it is the case that good marital and relationship function is associated with psychological and physical health, then, conversely, the breakdown of relationships and sexual dissatisfaction will impact on the couple's health. Current trends show a slight increase in older people divorcing. Remarriage is also more frequent at all ages (Weeks 2002). It is therefore likely that even when older couples have significant problems, it is to their advantage to help them deal with their problems to maximise their health.

Depression is the most common adult psychological problem, but one that affects the ageing patient even more than in earlier life. The most severe depressions occur in the sixth decade of life, and can be triggered by major losses, e.g. bereavement, loss of physical or sexual function, reduced social role or marital distress, or dysfunction (Champion 2000). Women are twice as likely as men to suffer depression, but men appear to suffer more severely in the event of marital breakdown. Depression is highly prevalent in the over-65s and will often go undiagnosed despite the fact that treatment is just as effective in old age as in younger age groups.

Anxiety about dementia often overshadows the incidence of depression in older people. Differential diagnosis between depression and dementia is often needed as the clinical presentation can be similar; the treatments could hardly be more different. Untreated depression may go some way to explaining the high rates of suicide among older people (Fennell 1989).

Carer depression

The most likely carer for the elderly or dying patient is the spouse or sexual partner. Many studies have found that care-giving wives tend to report higher levels of emotional distress and are more at risk of depression than care-giving husbands (Wright and Aquilino 1998). Reciprocal emotional support between elderly care-giving wives and their husbands who received care was linked to lower levels of care-giving burden and higher levels of marital happiness for wives (One Plus One 1998). The effects varied according to the husband's degree of disability, the positive effects decreasing as the level of disability increased. Among non-caregivers the level of mutual emotional support was also related to higher marital satisfaction. The findings suggest that interventions to increase care-giving wives' wellbeing should include enhancing the exchange of mutual emotional support. There is limited data to show that the length of the partnership will positively impact on the capacity of the carer to cope and sustain affectional bonds with the patient.

Elder abuse

The critical factors affecting the likelihood of elder abuse between spouses are the quality and length of the marital relationship, the nature of the diagnosis and the carer's perception of burden.

Violence in a partnership can present itself at the very end of a long partnership, especially when one becomes ill and the carer begins to perceive caring as burdensome. Sometimes it occurs as a manifestation of a previously dysfunctional marriage. It may be that the roles of abuser and victim become reversed when the illness strikes the abuser and makes the abuser vulnerable. The victim has unresolved anger and shows this by neglecting and/or abusing the perpetrator. A long-term marriage does not necessarily indicate a happy one and health professionals will have many opportunities to listen for and understand how illness in later life releases inhibitions – for both patient and partner.

John Bayley describes caring for his wife Iris Murdoch, in her final months of dementia:

> She knows the violence that is in me at moments and is just controlled, but only just. When I have been struggling for minutes at a time to get arms through sleeves or heels into shoes, she can feel that surge of ungentleness very close to the surface. Once she put her hands over her head and whimpered, 'Don't hit me.' She knew better than I did what might happen. (Bayley 2000)

Dementia

The main mental illness associated with older people, and feared by members of the public, is dementia. This condition, which is particularly distressing for relatives and carers, can result in a wide variety of altered behaviours. Department of Health figures suggest that around 600,000 people in Great Britain have a dementing illness. In fact, only 5–7 per cent of the population over 65 years suffer from some form of dementia. This, however, increases to 13 per cent at 80–84 years and to as much as 25 per cent in the 85+ age bracket. More women than men suffer the illness because they live longer than men. Thus male victims are more likely to be cared for by their partners; women are more likely to suffer alone or be cared for in residential settings.

Most people with dementia are cared for in their own homes. Woods (2001) has shown that the pre-morbid relationship, in terms of closeness and affection, is positively related to reduced caregiver strain and increased attitudes of affection. John Bayley, again writing about his wife, recalls: 'Even in the midst of the poor darling's endless agitations – banging on the front windows to alert passers-by, jerking endlessly at the locked front door, carrying clothes and cutlery round the house – there does seem to remain a core of serenity, in her smile, in the response to a tease, which I can't find anywhere in myself' (Bayley 2000).

Baikie (2002) reviews many of the themes and problems facing couples afflicted by dementia. Most dementia studies tend to focus on the negative aspects, such as reduced shared activities, loss of emotional support from the spouse, loss of decision-making, affection, sexual activity and a loss in the quality of verbal communication between partners (Wright 1993). Some studies have shown the very specific impact of dementia on affected partners in reducing their ability to provide practical and emotional support to the partner who gives care. It appears that women carers suffer this loss more than their male counterparts.

Another theme is that of the social death of the sick partner. Here studies have found three factors: the anticipation of the sufferer's death; the sufferer's lack of awareness of and response to the environment; and the carer's belief that the affected partner was in some ways already dead and that biological death would come as a relief. Social death does not occur at once, but rather comes with the gradual change in the sufferer's personality and the inability even to recognise the other, with just occasional glimpses of the previous self to remind the carer of what has been lost (Gilhooly et al. 1994).

The burden of caring

Carers vary in their responses. Pre-morbid marriages that are perceived by carers as equitable and affectionate are likely to result in less subjective strain. Carers consider the past: 'He was a good husband and father, and now it's my turn' or 'She would have done the same for me if I had been ill'. Partners who are carers remain faithful to their marriage vows and view their partner with compassion and love: 'He did not ask for this'.

Another strategy involves the idealisation of the relationship by the unaffected partner. Marital idealisation of the relationship is a good predictor of the reduced amount of burden a carer spouse will experience with a demented spouse. Idealisation is not associated with other types of self-deception, nor is it connected to trying to achieve social desirability. Rather, it is a separate activity that provides some distance between the partners.

Another distancing occurs when partners 'become' carers as well as spouses. They then access a wider world of voluntary organisations, other carers, state benefits and an identified and valued occupational role in society.

In conclusion, spouses see their role differently from other carer groups, and this is particularly the case in dementia. Men differ from women in their approach to caring. Men prefer a hands-on practical approach; women are better at sharing the emotional burden. We need to see dementia not just as a medical disorder, but also as a major disruption and stress within an intimate and dynamic relationship.

Sexual needs

There is a widely held belief amongst the public and some health professionals that sexuality is a function that declines with age, and that it is improper or inappropriate for the very old to have sexual needs or to express them. Older heterosexual women, especially widows, are perceived as 'sexless'. This can mean any or all of the following: not being sexually desirable, not being desirous of sex and not being sexually capable (Benbow and Jagus 2002). Trudel, Turgeon and Piche (2000) have demonstrated that sex is in fact one of the last drives to decline. They cite Kaplan (1990), who asserted that sexual response continues until death, but that the intensity, frequency and quality of that response is affected by age. Power-Smith (1991) summarises many of the physical illnesses that can indirectly affect sexual function: deafness interferes with intimate communication; osteoarthritis can make intercourse painful; colostomies, catheters and continence difficulties lead to couples sleeping apart and sometimes feeling ashamed or fearful of 'being dirty'. Stroke patients fear sex will lead to another attack, and they are reluctant to discuss this with health professionals. Older couples are often taking medication for a range of health issues that may reduce libido or interfere with sex drive.

Notwithstanding all this, older people can and do have sexual relations and benefit enormously from them in preserving physical and psychological wellbeing (Trudel, Turgeon and Piche 2000). All too often carers in residential and nursing homes do not acknowledge that older people continue to have a sex drive. This can lead to older people having their rights to privacy denied. All practitioners need to work sensitively with older people in expressing their sexuality.

Lack of social contact

During and after the death of the spouse, the wellbeing of the surviving party will critically depend on their capacity to make new social relationships, and on relationships that were developed prior to and during the caring. A wider social network appears to confer some of the benefits that a marriage does to the surviving partner and is itself a predictor of their capacity to form future partnerships or remarry.

Dementia involves the loss of partner before death. Here, the partner and children will express emotional distress long before their care recipient dies. Levels of affection within the marriage and satisfaction with the relationship were found to be inversely related to the amount of grief symptoms expressed by the caring spouse.

Saying goodbye

The final illness of the partner is an unsure and complex process, not least when both parties have significant health problems, and each will express anxiety about how the other half will cope 'once I'm gone'. Couples who have always communicated well and faced other bereavements as a shared experience will be better prepared to make their farewells and ensure that their affairs are properly in order. Children and health professional may be coerced into secretive alliances by each party, unable to share openly with the other that they are about to part.

Bereavement and loss

Any loss of a partner is considered to be one of the greatest human losses and we have words in English to denote the state of widowhood. Couples with health problems in old age have had more opportunity to prepare for loss than those who are widowed by accident or illness earlier in the lifecycle. This does not mean that the bereavement will run a smooth course. Grief is experienced more acutely when the relationship has been an unhappy or ambivalent one, and also if the couple have not faced loss before (Murray Parkes 1986).

If your patient dies, the bereaved partner will need support not just from you, but from the wider community. Older people who have spiritual beliefs and personal meaning are less likely to suffer mental health problems, even after the loss of a spouse.

Case study

You have established a relatives' support group for the sufferers of stroke in your district stroke unit. Most of the carers there are the partners of the patients who have all been assessed and treated in the inpatient part of the unit, and most patients and partners are in their sixties or seventies. One of the regular attenders, Joan, has begun to miss meetings and, despite your attempts to make contact, she is unable or unwilling to return.

You receive a letter from Joan, explaining that she finds coming to the group increasingly stressful because she feels deeply guilty in her role as primary caregiver. Far from obtaining support, Joan sees the group as critical of her and talking about her behind her back.

At first you cannot recall anything that the group might have said to give offence, but then you remember an incident a month earlier when she spoke candidly in the group about her unfulfilled sexual needs. Clearly there were other carers who sympathised and shared similar difficulties in caring for a patient with stroke. But not all the group felt this way; some couples had come to an understanding about how they expressed sexual affection, either through non-penetrative sex or through other types of physical affection.

You decide to reply to Joan and arrange to see her on a one-to-one basis, at least to provide her with the opportunity to express herself without the group and also without her partner. She expresses deep shame at even having sexual needs at the age of 74, and feels even more guilty that she is unable to speak to her partner George about her needs, as she feels his burden is greater than hers. When George was well, their sexual life had been balanced, and George had always been considerate to Joan during pregnancy and occasional illnesses. Joan now believes that she needs to abstain from all sexual contact with George, and sees even the invitation to discuss the matter as putting undue pressure on George to 'perform'.

For the first time she expresses the idea that George would like some kind of physical intimacy. She recognises her greatest fear; that any sexual exertion by George may trigger another stroke or even cause sudden death. The consequence for Joan has been that even when George has made a gesture of affection, she has quickly rebuffed it for fear of precipitating a crisis.

You wonder whether or not this fear has been expressed within the relationship. Joan says that it has not, but she does sense that George has a similar fear and she feels this might be the right time to discuss it with him. For the first time, you are in a position to remind her that the stroke unit staff can be approached for more information about sexual activity and stroke. She agrees to consider this with George.

Case study

Bill, aged 80, nursed his wife Gladys for the last year of her life when she was suffering from ovarian cancer. He has been bereaved for eight months. He attends your surgery complaining of poor sleep and appetite and you recognise that he is in danger of becoming clinically depressed. He had been offered support through CRUSE (see p. 139), but declined and has few friends or members of his immediate family in whom he can confide. You see that there is not enough time in the clinic to listen to all that he has to say, and immediately offer him a longer consultation before you make any decisions about treatment or referral to any specialist service. On the second consultation you notice a change in his mood. Bill expresses exasperation that his wife confided in her many female relatives and friends about her fears of cancer, and especially how it was affecting her marriage. But she did not talk about it with him, as 'she didn't want to upset him'. Bill is distressed and in two minds. Part of him was actually very frightened by his wife's illness, which he saw as silent and insidious, and he did not want to talk about it. Instead, he kept busy by providing physical care and reassuring Gladys that she would 'pull through'. He now worries that he did too much of the wrong thing. The other part of him was aching to discuss his fears with Gladys, and he was envious of the many friendships she had and the ease with which she spoke about 'affairs of the heart'. The whole unfinished business has left Bill feeling that he missed something important with Gladys, and that it is now too late to tell her how he feels.

You are aware of Bill's grief and relative isolation. You listen in detail to all he has to say and interject with questions, such as: 'What would Gladys say if she were sitting here beside you?' Finally, you wonder whether or not Bill would like to write a letter to Gladys, expressing all the hopes and fears and many affections that he had expressed. He is able to do this, and eventually works out that he would like to read it aloud at her graveside.

Guidelines for good practice

- Practitioners can encourage the patient as well as the partner to offer explicit affection, sympathy, empathy and respect to each other. The relationship is better maintained if the emotional support is balanced, even if physical tasks and care cannot be.
- Health professionals can encourage the older couple to talk to each other. Discourage secrets from their next of kin. Partners who declare

that they are trying to protect the feelings of their loved one can be gently challenged, as it is often the carers who are frightened of pain or loss and who project this fear onto their partners.

- Health professionals who listen need also to be able to give permission for expression of negative feelings. The anger or frustration of the patient and care-giving partner needs to be acknowledged and held, just as much as the good feelings about the partnership in the past. Active listening makes it safe for the partner to have these feelings and allows the carer to get back in touch with 'the good stuff'.
- Health professionals can work sensitively with the sexual needs of older couples better if they address their own assumptions and prejudices. Older people do not suddenly lose their sex drive. They need intimate contact with their partner to maintain their wellbeing. The medical and nursing staff working with elderly people should give higher priority to these needs in care planning.
- Health professionals should involve the spouse in care planning and discharge planning from hospital. Special consideration needs to be given to respite care and to offering dates that suit the spouse, rather than those that occur in hospital as opportunistic vacancies.
- Health visitors and district nurses who come to the home need to be sensitive to the stress of the burden of care on the carer and the risk of elder abuse. Remember that abuse can occur in both partners. It can be subtle and may not reflect the previous power relationships that existed in the partnership prior to illness.
- The health professional can give permission to the parties to disclose abuse: 'Looking after a partner can be so frustrating. Have you ever felt so bad you wanted to shout at/hit her?' It is essential that the professional is non-judgemental when counselling, as the partner is unlikely to disclose if reprimands rather than support are all that is offered.
- Partners in later life often have health needs themselves. These may be sidelined or completely overlooked, either by the couple or by practitioners who grow dependent on the support provided by the healthy partner. Vigilance and curiosity about the partner's wellbeing is appropriate and good practice. Carers have communication and compliance issues also and will require additional support and help in their role in treatment and rehabilitation.
- Remember that adjustment to bereavement is determined in part by the survivor's spiritual beliefs. It is good practice to ensure that they are reminded to maintain contact with their faith communities.

CHAPTER 10

Endings and Referring the Couple On

Introduction

This book has been about encouraging health professionals to work with patients' and their partners' relationships in medical settings. It has also been about empowering patients to use their relationship for health gain and maintenance. Much of what has been described has been about initial engagement and the establishment of a working alliance with the couple. The process of ending and disengagement from the couple requires equal consideration, especially when you may be continuing in your health role with your patient. You will be resuming a more familiar professional role, and it will be helpful for all if there is a common understanding about your future involvement. Endings are in part determined by the task that was begun with the couple and what an intervention was aimed at achieving. Endings may also be determined by the abilities of the practitioner to work well with the couple in the time available, and by underlying difficulties in the relationship that have coexisted with the illness, or are an integral part of it.

There will come a time, therefore, when the practitioner recognises either that the work has been done and disengagement is needed, or that more needs to be done for the couple and that a referral to another agency may be desirable. If a practitioner recognises she has neither the time, expertise nor departmental resources, then a referral to another service will be essential. Clinicians need a clear sense of their professional and personal boundaries for working with patients and partners in order for them to make a decision to refer on. The decision to refer on will generally be made after consideration of the nature of the problem, as well as its seriousness and urgency. Clinicians have a primary responsibility to recognise the limits of their competence.

Research findings into the area of referral to mental health services provide some insights into the factors likely to improve consultation and referral (Ross and Hardy 1999). These include: training in communication skills to improve the confidence of health practitioners (Ustun and Gater 1994); training in the use of brief counselling skills in consultations (Barker et al. 1990); the provision of screening instruments (Dowrick 1992); the development of formalised guidelines on appropriate treatment options (Hendryx, Doebbeling and Kearns 1994); and information on the nature and quality of support agencies for referral.

Endings and disengagement

Unless there has been an untoward event, a premature change in your patient's health status or a breakdown in your alliance with the couple, you will need some agreement on closure. There is little in the literature about this phase of your work (Schroeder 1997), which is surprising, given the level of anxiety that the couple may experience when the professional leaves them or refers them elsewhere. The couple have to face loss and separation from the health practitioner, just as in some situations they have to face the break-up and loss of their life together as a couple.

According to Schroeder (1997), there are two types of ending in the field of counselling, which represent different ends of a spectrum and within which you will find your own best practice. The first of these is the absolute position. This implies a referral on will mean you will not be seeing the couple again in a counselling context. Couples may have to face issues of failure and deprivation in an abrupt way. The other model is more graded, what Schroeder calls a 'health maintenance' model, where you will refer on and start to counsel the couple less. Termination of your relationship with patient and partner is thus provisional and protects the couple to some extent from the losses described above. You will need to work out an agreement that is appropriate to the physical and mental health of the patient, and to the nature of that illness. Clinicians will be influenced by the continuity of their caring role with the patient. What matters is that endings are planned for and discussed with the couple and, when appropriate, your supervisor or manager.

Endings consist of completion of the therapeutic task by the couple, and the provision of mutual feedback between the clinician and the couple about how well this has been achieved. Once progress has been reviewed, decisions can be made about ending the alliance. We recognise that health practitioners may have only had one or two contacts with the couple. In some situations, difficulties may have been discussed with the patient only. Limited contact can still achieve considerable relief and progress. Some clinicians may offer to see the couple in a follow-up visit. Others will decide to decrease contact in an agreed way, or to refer on.

Clinicians may underestimate their impact on the patient and partner, and the effect of loss in ending counselling. It is helpful for the couple to be involved in the discussion and agreement about ending. There may also be opportunities to recognise unfinished business that has been alluded to, but could be addressed in a referral (d'Ardenne and Mahtani 1999). Saying goodbye does not mean that couples have resolved all their problems; rather, the couple have come to a position where they are ready to face their world better prepared than when they first sought help.

The decision to refer on

The impulse to refer on may arise quite early in a consultation, but nevertheless needs to be contained. Practitioners have to make a decision in the light of their competence and capacity to support patients and their partners. You should also consider the quality of interdisciplinary working, consultation and support you can expect, and the availability and knowledge of local resources. Professionals may feel more confident dealing with couple difficulties if they receive support or guidance from colleagues, who may also reveal fresh or alternative routes for referral. There will also be times when, however confident you feel to support the couple, you may have to face your limited time resource, and refer on.

The process of referral includes decisions about when to refer on, which patients to refer on, which other professionals or agency are accessible and whether a formal or informal referral is advisable. It helps to share this information in a caring and confident way with the couple as early in the consultation as the decision is made.

It is worth avoiding a hasty decision and allowing enough of the story to unfold to get a sense of the patients' need.

The 'pinch-crunch' model of conflict (Grimer 1987) may clarify the decision and provide a useful yardstick. In this model, couples are described as being at a 'pinch' when a period of stability and commitment is eroded by unresolved issues. At this stage, couples are accessible to help and change, and may need a modest intervention, to improve communication for example. Couples who fail to deal with these inevitable 'pinches' build up to a situation where both partners know that something is seriously awry. Here, the couple have reached what Grimer (1987) describes as the 'crunch' stage, which may well need expert intervention. If the practitioner remains unsure, it may be useful to offer further contact. The couple may then be less agitated and able to consider the need for referral clearly.

Recognisable stages of referral for practitioners include the initial help seeking of the patient, exploration of the difficulty, assessment of the problem, the decision to refer and finally the referral. The clinical skills for referring couples on include all the listening skills used in inviting disclosure and exploring the couple's initial difficulties. Practitioners who possess these skills are more likely to disengage skilfully and facilitate re-engagement of the couple in the referral process.

Referring on will also be influenced by your knowledge of the couple and their social circumstances. You have to establish the willingness and motivation of the couple to take up the referral and have the capacity yourself to disengage. The suitability of the couple, and their attitude to counselling and support services, will be implicated in the decision. It is not unusual for a patient to be reluctant to attend counselling because of perceived stigma, lack of confidence or motivation. If the waiting list is too long or the cost or distance beyond the means of the couple, they are unlikely to follow through.

Referral pathways

Many couples self-refer where they have common knowledge of agencies such as marriage guidance organisations, or are following up suggestions from friends or relatives. In this situation, responsibility remains with the couple. Couples who make their own decision have already begun a process of communication and decision-making. The health professional, of course, may still enquire about progress and even incorporate it into their health care plan.

The couple may also respond to a suggestion by a health practitioner. According to a study carried out by One Plus One (Ayles and Reynolds 2001), the most common response in primary care was to suggest a service, usually Relate (previously, the National Marriage Guidance Council). The advantage of this pathway is that the couple themselves still take ownership of the decision. The health professional has little work to do by way of input to the referral, or from the referral. The disadvantage is that one partner, usually the man, may not be able or willing to go to a marriage support agency (Brannen and Collard 1982). Similarly, the absent partner may believe that the couple should be able to sort out their own problems – only couples with serious problems go for marriage guidance! When the professional makes contact with a colleague or another agency by letter or telephone call, a more formal and direct process of referral has been initiated. The professional may be required to follow through with further information.

Direct referrals offer liaison and communication, but will also require you to write a letter of referral or at least to fill in a referral form outlining the nature of the difficulty for the couple, and what you might like to be done for them. Ideally forms should be straightforward and brief, but it is not always the case. It remains time well spent, however, in caring for your patient and partner. You may need to get financial clearance for this if you are within a Health Trust that has limited funds and places a lower priority on the needs of the couple than on the family.

Some of you may not be able to refer directly at all. You may have to seek permission or guidance from the holder of health funds to make a formal referral. Examples of fund holders include the family doctor, a consultant physician or a head of a health department. In such cases you may be required to provide a convincing rationale for the referral and expense. Professionals are more likely to make an effective referral if they know the criteria for referral and the aims and ethics of the chosen agency or local counselling service. It is also wise to try to establish the theoretical base of the agency, and approximately how long assessments and interventions take.

Referring on to couple therapy

Couples who are able to own the decision and take part in the planning are good candidates for referral. Patients and partners who have enough insight to recognise that their difficulties do not reside entirely in physical symptoms are likely to fare better. Likewise, couples who are motivated to change their relationship and who believe it is possible to change their relationship are likely to do better. Other criteria include: those who are not embarrassed to talk about their relationship issues; those who have some language to describe emotion and their experience of change in emotional wellbeing; and couples who have a strong emotional and cultural affinity with the health professional.

Counsellors may offer guidance about patients they will accept. They name couples who are motivated and open to change, have problems of a shorter duration and couples who do not have a split agenda. Couples who are struggling with plans or goals for the future may benefit. Some agencies suggest that unsuitable clients include those with psychiatric problems, problems with violence, alcohol or substance abuse or medically based problems. There is little in the field on referring patients with relationship problems to specialist services. However Ayles and Reynolds (2001) carried out an in-depth qualitative study which we shall now discuss in some detail.

The study explored the attitudes and experiences of health professionals and counselling services to managing patients with relationship problems. In particular, the study examined when and how patients are referred on for counselling. Some patients readily turn to practitioners for help, but there were others who find it difficult and would often not reveal their difficulties for some time. This latter group included older patients, many men and people who were less open, or who felt too embarrassed to ask directly for help. They also included those from different cultural backgrounds from the health professional, those who do not expect help or do not expect it to make a difference, and those patients who more commonly present with physical symptoms such as headaches, abdominal pain, sleep disturbance and low energy.

The most common disclosure of relationship problems was in response to open questions about general wellbeing. More direct enquiries from the professional tended to follow cues from the patient or might be prompted by their behaviour or appearance. It was unusual for a patient to admit difficulties. It was more likely that an allusion to difficulties would be made rather than a direct disclosure. A number of meetings may be necessary to build trust and a sense of acceptance before a couple feel able to reveal any problems.

Key findings from the study

Barriers to referral for counselling

A clearly defined difficulty in referring on was the very limited knowledge of local counselling services and knowledge of available services was obtained unsystematically. Most health professionals would like more information, including the methods and qualifications of counsellors. Knowledge of services and counsellors' working methods was scant and seemed to be owing to chance. Counsellors themselves thought that the lack of widely agreed standards and guidelines was potentially damaging to the reputation and practice of counselling. As one CPN said in the study, 'I don't feel comfortable in recommending places that I'm not personally aware of'. Direct referral to counsellors in primary care was rare, except where a base was shared, usually in a GP practice. Private counsellors were not recommended because of lack of information and concern over standards. Professionals felt uncomfortable recommending support when they were not personally aware of the resource. Generally, they viewed counselling positively but it was not necessarily thought to be the most suitable option. Making a decision to refer was mainly dictated by the reputation of a service and familiarity with what was on offer.

There was very little contact between health professionals and counsellors. Professionals rarely knew whether patients had taken up counselling or what the outcome of any attendance had been. Issues of confidentiality created difficulties for counsellors and created barriers to contact with the professional. One nurse who recognised the confidentiality barrier expressed her desire to know how patients were getting on and the couple's willingness to discuss their progress with them when they came to see her. Professionals and counsellors would generally prefer greater collaboration, but the barriers mentioned and lack of personal information prevented this happening.

Contradictions in confidentiality

A private counsellor in the study observed: 'There is an inherent tension between the client's need to control their own information (confidentiality) and the need for good referrals and feedback.'

Health professionals are educated to assess and treat patients and communicate their clinical work to their colleagues within the team or even larger healthcare systems. Maintenance of shared health records is a key component to effective, ongoing care of the patient. Confidentiality within this culture means that information in the case record may be accessed by those who have a responsibility for that person's care. In the UK, this is enshrined in the Access to Medical Records Act 1990.

In contrast, counsellors are educated to value privacy, individuality and the personal relationship. Record-keeping varies between counsellors and counselling organisations. Confidentiality between the counsellor and the client is sacrosanct, and information is not usually shared with the referrer or the client's family. Where referral is made to a counsellor by a health professional, feedback is rarely known and not usually expected. As one practice nurse said, 'I suppose there is that confidentiality barrier there... but it would be nice to know how they're getting on and when they come to see me, I can discuss it with them.'

The part played by the couple

Clinicians need to understand the part the couple play in an effective referral. Their co-operation and motivation will be influenced not just by their experience of working with you, but also by their experience of other kinds of help offered and taken in the past. Their attitude to support and their previous experience of outside help will influence their co-operation and their compliance, just as it has in their dealings with you. You will be ideally placed to judge this and to provide some straightforward feedback about how much will be required of them. For example, although couple counselling may be the preferred route, it is very common for one partner to be reluctant to attend, leaving the other with a sense of abandonment at the referral stage and wanting to know whether or not to attend therapy alone. Part of making the decision entails an assessment of the barriers to either party and a thinking through of the implications of refusal for both of them. Another part of that decision involves the level of contact, if any, that the couple will wish to maintain with you whether or not the referral is taken up.

Wider options for the couple

Referring on may include a wide range of options which you can select and discuss with your patient and partner. The range extends from immediate family and friends to peer/self-help groups to counselling to specialist psychotherapy or psychiatry. Couples vary enormously in the way they perceive services as acceptable or stigmatising. Some couples will feel comfortable about being referred to a counsellor or counselling psychologist within a hospital department or within a primary healthcare setting. It may be that one or both partners are showing sufficient distress to refer to a community mental health team or a department of psychiatry. Others will have the confidence to share their problems with a trusted pastor, relative or friend.

Practitioners should be able to access an up-to-date and comprehensive resource list of referral agencies, some of which we have included at the end of this book. You and your colleagues also need to maintain a list of local neighbourhood resources. This includes agencies that may be more culturally appropriate to a couple and their healthcare needs.

Couples benefit from socialisation, information, skill acquisition, leisure and fun, further education and physical activity. As counselling does not suit everyone, help can be found in surprising places. Good examples include mental health organisations such as the National Schizophrenia Fellowship, MIND (National Association for Mental Health), as well as Home-Start, Gingerbread, the Citizens' Advice Bureau, Alcoholics Anonymous and the National Society for the Prevention of Cruelty to Children. Support can also be provided indirectly by sports and leisure centres, churches, adult education facilities, parents' groups and toddlers' clubs.

Self-help groups or peer groups may be more acceptable to some people than counselling services. Some clients are reluctant to join groups because they lack confidence or feel inadequate. Others prefer the attention of a one-to-one situation. It is realistic to consider other sources of help available to the patient or couple such as supportive family and friends, new activities and interests, websites, videos, films and books. The practitioner who has a working relationship with the referral agency and understands what is on offer will be more confident and more successful in selecting and 'selling' a referral to the couple.

What if the couple do not go?

A referral that is not taken up by the couple can complicate your relationship with them and can also create frustration and anxiety in you. What happens, for example, if one or both partners of the couple refuse to attend specialist treatment or counselling? How hard do you push, and how much of this can be foreseen at the beginning of the referral process? Under what circumstances would you insist that some other specialist sees your patient. However skilful the referral process, couples still default, and an understanding of their experience is desirable. It may be that you have provided all the support that the couple needed, or that the timing was wrong, perhaps for practical reasons – financial, transport or childcare – or psychological reasons – unconscious fears of loss or anger with the therapist or partner.

Alternatively, the couple may not have reached a time in their lives when they are ready or able to face the challenge that disclosure and possible change create.

A more worrying concern is when couples who may be at risk (self-harm or harm to others) or are vulnerable to exploitation do not attend. Practitioners should record their referral in the patient's notes, discuss the risks with their supervisor/manager and ensure that local policies regarding risk management have been observed. The family doctor should also be appraised of the situation, and as much of your concerns recorded in writing as is practical.

Case study

You are a nurse specialist in a department of dermatology and have a patient, Donna, with psoriasis, which flares up every time she has arguments with her fifteen-year-old son. You have already provided a great deal of support to this family and helped her work out for herself how to reduce stress and manage her symptoms on a day-to-day basis. Donna has suffered lifelong low self-esteem and you are aware that her husband Jim, a likeable man, is supportive and caring, and regularly attends the clinic with her.

Donna arrives one day in tears, after what you believe to have been an argument with her son. You are surprised to hear her blurt out that Jim has moved out of the family home, after he has admitted having a fling with another woman. Although he does not want to continue with the affair, he does not want to return home. Donna is humiliated. She explains that Jim has always found her physical symptoms difficult and that sexual attraction has been undermined a great deal by this. You are less convinced, and think that the skin condition is being blamed for deeper tensions within the marriage, which have had no expression. You ask her how much talking has actually taken place between Jim and herself, but she appears unable and unwilling to discuss it further. You become aware that the difficulties in this relationship and their interaction with Donna's symptoms are inaccessible to you.

You ask Donna if she or Jim has ever considered counselling or therapy. She expresses many fears about therapy, but accepts that she could talk in another setting. You reassure her first of all that she will remain your patient for as long as her condition requires it. You also explain about confidentiality and that she can refer herself and/or her husband to a marriage guidance organisation without any intervention from you. You further explain that you can refer herself and her husband for relationship therapy at a nearby specialised service, and that she will now need to talk with Jim and consider some of these choices in more detail.

Case study

You are a district nurse caring for James who suffers from advanced bowel disease. While you are visiting him, it becomes clear that there are problems between James and his partner, Elizabeth. She has definite ideas about the origins of the illness and its management on a day-to-day basis. James is less sure and more passive in his response to the disease, which has had a devastating effect on his capacity to work, earn money or play an active role in parenting their three daughters. Elizabeth is always at the house when you come to change James's dressings, and this couple disagree about all these matters increasingly in your presence.

You begin to worry about the effect of all this on James's capacity to respond to treatment and his self-esteem. You perceive Elizabeth as needy, but also invasive and you grow increasingly resentful of what you see as her intrusions into your treatment. After discussion in supervision, you decide that it would be better to refer this couple on for some simple counselling around their differences with a counsellor attached to James's GP practice.

You raise the issue with the couple. James's immediate response is to ask whether or not your visits to the house are likely to cease as a result of this referral. You are able to reassure him about this and indicate that it will be 'business as usual' as far as your involvement with his care is concerned. You suggest a gradual phasing out of contact with Elizabeth, which starts by her being present at all your visits, but that the frequency and duration of contact with you will be gradually reduced as she and James get to see more of the counsellor.

Information about services and resources

These are listed in the Resource List at the back of the book, but can only be a starting point for referral on. Our list, however, is no substitute for your knowledge and confidence in local services. You might like to keep your own resource folder on which agencies, services and people are available to help couples. National and local services change their addresses, web-sites and service remit, and your folder will need to be regularly updated.

Ask your patient and partner what they know about and have found interesting or appropriate to their needs. If you find yourself referring frequently to a particular agency, it might be more beneficial and straightforward to visit them in person and obtain a more direct picture of the content and style of their work, and the kind of people who work there. It will also enable you to reassure the couples you are referring on, based on your direct observation.

Lastly, we would encourage you to accept that some couples will readily move on and address their difficulties. However, personal change can be difficult and slow. There will be a surprising range of responses to intervention – some apparently very small, some unpredictable. There will always be couples who will not take this opportunity and they will take final responsibility for their own wellbeing. As you grow in confidence working with couples, you will become more realistic about counselling couples in healthcare and satisfied by what can be achieved.

Guidelines for good practice

(based on One Plus One 2001)
- Establish your supervision and management relationships and your model of work (Shipton 1997).
- Attend to those who may 'slip through the net'. Prepare a strategy that will allow you to track these patients and follow them up if they fail to attend your clinic or that of the agency you have referred them to.
- Address relationship problems systematically in clinical practice to enable discharge and referral to another agency to occur in a low key, routine way.
- Respond to signals of distress. It is only through a raised awareness of the couple's distress and the skills of reflecting back to the couple, that you can facilitate this initial phase of getting the help they are seeking.
- Remember that practitioners also give signals about how busy or open they are, how much they care, or how judgemental their attitude is.
- Do not pursue the issue if patients are unwilling to share their

problems with you, and see this domain as the one which may need to be shared with the couple therapist.

- Keep in touch with yourself. Being aware of your feelings provides valuable clues about the couple, your relationship with them, your own barriers to referral and your personal competence. Use your regular supervision sessions for these issues.
- Review regularly – check with the couple how they see their progress.
- Involve the couple in deciding when they have had enough contact with you.
- Explore with the couple what they have tried in the past that they have found beneficial. This will give you a clue as to the kind of help they are likely to seek in the future, and likely to stay with.
- Do not be frightened of acknowledging when you can no longer assist the couple directly.
- Check out information on local service providers, and visit them. You are unlikely to follow up cues if you expect to get out of your depth and have no idea as to where to send the couple for help.
- Seek information on how support services operate, what they provide and the criteria for making referrals.
- Agree what information can be shared with different professionals.
- Encourage contact with local support services. Why not invite them to meet your team? Personal contact oils the wheels of a good referral.
- Provide materials, leaflets or information about the service or group recommended.
- Remember the value of mutual support from other colleagues and disciplines. Make sure you attend and promote multidisciplinary team meetings.
- Consider how to respond sensitively to couples who default. Going for special help is never easy; it creates a sense of stigma and requires a great deal of trust.
- Seek out training to increase skills and confidence.

Resource List

Health

Age Concern England
Astral House
1268 London Road
London SW16 4ER
Tel: 020 8765 7200 Fax: 020 8765 7211
Information Line: 0800 009966
www.ageconcern.org.uk

Age Concern is a large charitable movement in the UK concerned with the needs and aspirations of older people and the leading authority on ageing-related issues.

Alzheimer's Society
Gordon House
10 Greencoat Place
London SW1P 1PH
Tel: 020 7306 0606 Fax: 020 7306 0808
www.alzheimers.org.uk

The Alzheimer's Society is a leading UK care and research charity for people with any form of dementia and their carers.

Arthritis Care
18 Stephenson Way
London NW1 2HD
Tel: 020 7380 6500 Fax: 020 7380 6505
www.arthritiscare.org.uk

Arthritis Care is a leading, UK-wide, voluntary organisation working with and for all people with arthritis.

Black Health Agency

Zion Community Centre
339 Stretford Road
Hulme
Manchester M15 4ZY
Tel: 0161 226 9145

Black Health Agency provides a range of health-related services and initiatives for the diverse black communities locally, regionally and nationally.

Breast Cancer Care

Kiln House
210 New Kings Road
London SW6 4NZ
Tel: 020 7384 2984 Free Helpline: 0808 800 6000
www.breastcancercare.org.uk

Breast Cancer Care is a leading provider of breast cancer information and support across the UK. Its services are free and include a helpline, web-site, publications and practical and emotional support.

British Society for Rheumatology

41 Eagle Street
London WC1R 4TL
Tel: 020 7242 3313 Fax: 020 7242 3277
www.rheumatology.org.uk for links to: professional bodies, patient groups and journals

The British Society for Rheumatology is the UK professional organisation for people working in rheumatology and related fields.

CancerBACUP

3 Bath Place
Rivington Street
London EC2A 3JR
Tel: 020 7696 9003 Fax: 020 7696 9002
www.cancerbacup.org.uk

CancerBACUP's mission is to give cancer patients and their families the up-to-date information, practical advice and support they need to reduce the fear and uncertainty of cancer.

Cancer Black Care

16 Dalston Lane
London E8 3AZ
Tel: 020 7249 1097 Fax: 020 7249 0606
www.cancerblackcare.org

Cancer Black Care offers support and help to all ethnic communities who are affected by cancer, including friends, carers or families.

Depression Alliance
35 Westminster Bridge Road
London SE1 7JB
Tel: 020 7633 0557 Fax: 020 7633 0559
www.depressionalliance.org

Depression Alliance is a UK charity offering help to people with depression.

Diabetes UK
10 Queen Anne Street
London W1M 0BD
Tel: 020 7323 1531 Fax: 020 7637 3644
www.diabetes.org.uk

Diabetes UK is a leading charity working for people with diabetes. It funds research, campaigns and helps people to live with the condition.

Headway – The Brain Injury Association
4 King Edward Court
King Edward Street
Nottingham NG1 1EW
Tel: 0115 924 0800 Fax: 0115 958 4446 Minicom: 0115 950 7825
www.headway.org.uk

Headway – The Brain Injury Association aims to promote understanding of all aspects of head injury and to provide information, support and services to people who have suffered a head injury, their family and carers.

The Impotence Association
PO Box 10296
London SW17 9WH
Helpline: 020 8767 7791
www.impotence.org.uk

The Impotence Association is a charitable organisation which helps sufferers of impotence (erectile dysfunction) and their partners and raises awareness of the condition amongst the public and the medical profession.

Issue (National Fertility Association)
114 Lichfield Street
Walsall WS1 1SZ
Tel: 01922 722888 Fax: 01922 640070
www.issue.co.uk

Issue provides fact sheets, books, articles and a regular magazine about infertility. It gives support through local contacts and provides telephone counselling by professional infertility counsellors.

Marie Curie Cancer Care
89 Albert Embankment
London SE1 7TP
Tel: 020 7599 7777
www.mariecurie.org.uk

Marie Curie cares for people affected by cancer and promotes the enhancement of the quality of their life through its services, research and education.

Mencap
123 Golden Lane
London EC1Y 0RT
Tel: 020 7454 0454 Fax: 020 7696 5540
www.mencap.org.uk for a web-based, A–Z index or links by county

Mencap provides a variety of services for people with a learning disability and their families and carers. This includes support with housing, education, employment and leisure activities.

Mind (The National Association for Mental Health)
15–19 Broadway
London E15 4BQ
MindinfoLine: 08457 660 163
www.mind.org.uk

Mind is one of the UK's leading mental health charities.

Multiple Sclerosis Society
MS National Centre
72 Edgware Road
London NW2 6ND
Tel: 020 8438 0700 Helpline: 0800 7833 157
www.mssociety.org.uk

The MS Society funds MS research, runs holiday homes and respite care, and provides grants, education and training on MS.

NSF (National Schizophrenia Fellowship)
Freepost
SEA9307
Southampton

NSF is a national organisation which provides information, campaigns and services to improve the lives for all those affected by mental illness.

Patient UK

Tel: 0191 217 1536 Fax: 0191 217 1536

www.patient.co.uk

Patient UK is a directory of health, disease and related web-sites from the UK. It is edited by Drs Tim and Beverley Kenny, who are general practitioners from Newcastle upon Tyne. Their stated aim is to direct non-medical people in the UK to good quality information about health and disease.

RADAR

12 City Forum

50 City Road

London EC1V 8AF

Tel: 020 7250 3222 Fax: 020 7250 0212 Minicom: 020 7250 4119

www.radar.org.uk for links to other resources from access to transport

The Royal Association for Disability and Rehabilitation (RADAR) is a national organisation of and for disabled people. One of its key areas of activity is supporting over 500 local and national disability organisations.

SCOPE

6 Market Road

London N7 9PW

Tel: 020 7619 7100 Helpline: 0808 800 3333

www.scope.org.uk

Scope is a disability organisation in England and Wales whose focus is people with cerebral palsy.

The Stroke Association

Stroke House

Whitecross Street

London EC1Y 8JJ

Tel: 020 7566 0300 Fax: 020 7490 2686 Helpline: 0845 30 33 100

www.stroke.org.uk

The Stroke Association is a national UK charity, which is solely concerned with stroke. It provides support for people who have had strokes, their families and carers.

The Terrence Higgins Trust

52–54 Gray's Inn Road

London WC1X 8JU

Tel: 020 7831 0330 Fax: 020 7242 0121

www.tht.org.uk

Terrence Higgins Trust (THT) is a leading HIV and AIDS charity in the UK and Europe.

Young Minds
102–108 Clerkenwell Road
London EC1M 5SA
Tel: 020 7336 8445 Fax: 020 7336 8446
www.youngminds.org.uk

Young Minds is a national charity committed to improving the mental health of all children. It provides leaflets and booklets, seminars, training and a consultancy service.

Counselling and couple support

Albany Trust
239 Balham High Road
London SW17 7BE
Tel: 020 8767 1827

Albany Trust is a charitable foundation providing one-to-one, couple and group counselling and psychotherapy, both short- and long-term. It specialises in psychosexual problems, sexual identity, sexual compulsion and gender identity. It also deals with issues arising from anxiety in relationships, bereavement and feelings of low self-worth.

African Caribbean Family Mediation Service
2–4 St John's Crescent
London SW9 7LZ
Tel: 020 7737 2366 Fax: 020 7733 0637
www.acfms.org

A south London-based service offering relationship counselling, child-focused mediation, a home/school mediation service and a counselling service for men.

Asian Family Counselling Service
Suite 51, Windmill Place
2–4 Windmill Lane
Southall UB2 4NJ
Tel/Fax: 020 8571 3933
Email: afcs99@hotmail.com

An organisation providing marriage preparation, marriage enrichment and counselling. It aims to advance education among people of Asian origin on all aspects of marriage and family relationships.

The Child Psychotherapy Trust
Star House
104–108 Grafton Road
London NW5 4BD
Tel: 020 7284 1355
www.childpsychotherapytrust.org.uk

A charity that works to improve access to appropriate child psychotherapy of children
and families in need of help.

Institute of Family Therapy
24–32 Stephenson Way
London NW1 2HX
Tel: 020 7391 9150 Fax: 0207 391 9169
www.instituteoffamilytherapy.org.uk

Marriage counselling, training, family therapy and communication skills.

Jewish Marriage Council
23 Ravenshurst Avenue
London NW4 4EE
Tel: 020 8203 6311 Fax: 020 8203 8727
www.jmc-uk.org

An organisation providing counselling for anyone under stress or with a problem concerning relationships. It offers advice and group discussion for engaged and newly
married couples.

London Marriage Guidance
76a New Cavendish Street
London W1G 9PE
Tel: 020 7580 1087 Fax: 020 7637 4546
www.londonmarriageguidance.org.uk

Individual and couple relationship counselling.

Marriage Care
1 Blythe Mews
Blythe Road
London W14 0NW
Tel: 020 7371 1341 Fax: 020 7371 4921
www.marriagecare.org.uk

Offers relationship counselling and preparation for marriage.

Marriage Care Scotland
10 Panmure Street
Dundee DD1 2BW
Tel: 01382 227 551

Relationship counselling for couples and individuals, pre-marriage work and education work.

Muslim Marriage Guidance Council
8 Caburn Road
Hove
Sussex BN3 6EF
24-hour contact line: 07971 861972

A service to help cross-cultural marriages and provide counselling. It offers services in a wide range of languages.

NAFSIYAT
Inter-Cultural Therapy Centre
278 Seven Sisters Road
London N4 2HY
Tel: 020 7263 4130
E-mail: nafsiyat-therapy@supanet.com

NAFSIYAT provides psychotherapy by therapists from a wide range of ethnic and cultural backgrounds for clients, individuals, families and adolescents, from diverse backgrounds. A wide range of languages is also available.

Partner Therapy Group
Tel: 07977 493 667
www.partnertherapy.com

A web-based advisory and self-referral service specialising in sexual and relationship problems. All practitioners are registered with the UK Council for Psychotherapy.

Relate (National Marriage Guidance)
Herbert Gray College
Little Church Street
Rugby CV21 3AP
Tel: 01788 573241
www.relate.org.uk

Offers counselling and individual relationship counselling through 100 local centres.

SPOD
286 Camden Road
London N7 0BJ
Tel: 020 7607 8851 Fax: 020 7700 0236
www.spod-uk.org

SPOD is a UK association that aids the sexual and personal relationships of people with a disability.

SSAFA (Soldiers' Sailors' and Airmen's Families Association)
19 Queen Elizabeth Street
London SE1 2LP
Tel: 020 7403 8783
www.ssafa.org.uk

Provides a welfare and advisory service for families of serving and ex-service men and women.

Stepfamily Scotland
5 Coates Place
Edinburgh EH3 7AA
Tel: 0131 225 8005 Fax: 0131 225 3514
www.stepfamilyscotland.org.uk

Support and information for all members of stepfamilies and those who work with them.

The Tavistock Marital Studies Institute
Tavistock Centre
120 Belsize Lane
London NW3 5BA.
Tel: 020 435 7111 Fax: 020 435 1080
www.tmsi.org.uk

The Institute is internationally recognised as a world leader in the psychoanalytic understanding of the couple relationship. It offers couple therapy and engages in research, training and consultations to the wider voluntary, health and statutory fields.

Westminster Pastoral Foundation
23 Kensington Square
London W8 5HN
Tel: 020 7361 4864 Fax: 020 7361 4860
www.wpf.org.uk

WPF is a large UK charitable provider of general counselling and psychotherapy services and psychodynamic counselling and psychotherapy training.

Family support

2as1.net
Tel: 0700 2222 700 Fax: 020 8659 6659
www.2as1.net

A new organisation primarily serving the black community in Britain. Provides a web-based information service for marriage and relationship support.

The Centre for Parent and Child Support
South London and Maudsley NHS Trust
Munro Centre
66 Snowsfields
London SE1 3SS
Tel: 020 7378 3235 Fax: 020 7378 3243
www.cpcs.org.uk

A centre for the improvement of parent and child support services and the promotion of family wellbeing and development via consultation, training and research.

Contact-a-Family
209–211 City Road
London E11V 1JN
Tel: 020 7608 8700 Fax: 020 7608 8701 Minicom: 020 7608 8702
Free helpline 0808 808 3555
www.cafamily.org.uk

Encourages mutual support between families in the same neighbourhood caring for children with a disability or special need. Over 800 local groups and contacts in the UK.

Cruse Bereavement Care
Cruse House
126 Sheen Road
Richmond-upon-Thames TW9 1UR
Tel: 020 8939 9530 Fax: 020 8940 7638 Helpline: 0870 167 1677
www.crusebereavement.org.uk

A large bereavement charity in the UK with 180 local branches offering free counselling, local support groups, practical advice and information.

The Family Nurturing Network
Ground Floor, Temple Court
109 Oxford Road
Oxford OX4 2ER
Tel: 01865 777756 Fax: 01865 777702
www.fnn.org.uk

A voluntary organisation providing parenting support and education to families with children with emotional and behavioural problems through a network of volunteers.

Family Welfare Association
501–505 Kingsland Road
London E8 4AU
Tel: 020 7254 6251 Fax: 020 7249 5443

Supports families to overcome the effects of poverty and runs family and children's centres across the UK.

Home-Start
2 Salisbury Road
Leicester LE1 7QR
Tel: 0116 233 9955 Fax: 0116 233 0232
www.home-start.org.uk

National network of 300 community-based groups offering support, friendship and practical help though volunteer parents to families with at least one child under five in their own homes.

Meet-a-Mum Association
Waterside Centre
26 Avenue Road
London SE25 4DX
Tel: 020 8771 5595 Fax: 020 8239 1153 Helpline: 020 8760 0123
www.mama.org.uk

Offers a listening ear to mothers suffering from postnatal illness and their families. Puts mothers feeling isolated after birth in contact with local MAMA groups and other mothers.

National Association of Citizens Advice Bureaux (NACAB)
Myddleton House
115–123 Pentonville Road
London N1 9LZ
www.nacab.org.uk
www.adviceguide.org.uk

Provides free, impartial and confidential advice and help thorough local bureaux to anybody on any subject, including legal and financial matters. There are 1,700 CAB offices and outlets throughout the UK.

National Family Mediation
9 Tavistock Place
London WC1H 9SN
Tel: 020 7383 5993 Fax: 020 7383 5994
www.nfm.u-net.com

Network of local services offering help to couples who are in the process of separation and divorce.

National Newpin
Sutherland House
35 Sutherland Square
London SE17 3EE
Tel: 020 7358 5900 Fax: 020 7701 2660
www.newpin.org.uk

A charity which supports parents under stress. Its seventeen centres offer individual counselling, peer support, training, workshops and an antenatal scheme.

NSPCC
42 Curtain Road
London EC2A 3NH
Tel: 020 7825 2500
www.nspcc.org.uk

National society for the prevention of cruelty to children.

One Plus One Marriage and Partnership Research
The Wells
7–15 Rosebery Avenue
London EC1R 4SP
Tel: 020 7841 3660 Fax: 020 7841 3670
www.oneplusone.org.uk for links to Springboard a membership scheme providing access to information and resources

One Plus One works closely with other marriage and family support organisations and has developed ground-breaking training and resources for those working with couples and their families.

Breastfeeding

La Leche League of Great Britain
PO Box 29
West Bridgford
Nottingham NG2 7NP
Telephone 24 hour helpline: 020 7242 1278
www.laleche.org.uk

Help for mothers who want to breastfeed.

National Childbirth Trust
Alexandra House
Oldham Terrace
London W3 6NH
Enquiry line: 0870 444 8707 Breast feeding line: 0870 444 8708
www.nctpregnancyandbabycare.com

The National Childbirth Trust is a registered charity and membership organisation providing a range of services including antenatal classes, postnatal discussion groups and breastfeeding counselling. It has a network of over 380 local branches.

Helplines

Al-non
24-hour confidential helpline: 020 7403 0888

Supports families and friends of problem drinkers.

Blackliners
Tel: 020 7738 5274

Black lesbian and gay HIV support.

Child Death Helpline
Free helpline: 0800 282986

A confidential listening service provided by Great Ormond Street Hospital's Child Death Helpline Department offering befriending and emotional support for all those affected by the death of a child.

Childline
Free 24-hour confidential help line 0800 1111

For children and young people in the UK.

Compassionate Friends (The)
Helpline: 0117 953 9639

A national organisation offering support and friendship for bereaved parents and their families by those similarly bereaved, by telephone, one-to-one contact or through local support groups.

Contact a Family
Free helpline: 0808 808 3555

For parents and families, encouraging mutual support between families caring for children with a disability or special needs.

Face to Face
Free helpline: 0808 800 3333

A joint project run by Scope and Mencap. Trained volunteers who are parents of disabled children support parents who have recently discovered their child has a disability.

Gay/Lesbian/Bisexual Helplines

24-hour helpline: 020 7837 7324 including minicom
www.queenscene.com/Gay_Scene/Helplines/helplines.html

Extensive web-site listings covering national, regional and local services including issues from alcoholism, bereavement, counselling and psychotherapy, disabilities, drugs, HIV and AIDS to rape.

Gingerbread
Free helpline: 0800 018 4318
www.gingerbread.org.uk

Offers help and support to lone parents through over 100 local groups.

Lone Parent Line
Free helpline: 0800 018 5026

Provided by the National Council for One Parent Families to promote the welfare of lone parents and their children.

Parentline Plus
Free 24-hour helpline: 0808 800 2222

National service for parents in distress. A free textphone helpline is also available.

Saneline
Helpline: 0845 767 8000

Support and information for sufferers and carers of people with mental illness.

Serene, incorporating the CRY-SIS helpline
Helpline: 020 7404 5011

Support for families with excessively crying or sleepless babies and youngsters.

THTDirect
Helpline: 0845 1221200

Information and support for people with HIV/Aids provided by the Terrence Higgins Trust.

Women's Aid National Domestic Violence Helpline
24-hour Helpline: 08457 023 468

Women's Aid Federation of England (Women's Aid) is the national charity working to end domestic violence against women and children.

Young Minds Parents' Information Line
Free helpline: 0800 018 2138

Offering information and support on young peoples' mental health for parents.

Professional practice

The British Association of Behavioural and Cognitive Psychotherapists
Globe Centre
PO Box 9
Accrington BB5 2GD
Tel: 01254 875277 Fax: 01254 239114
www.babcp.org.uk

Provision of directory of registered therapists.

British Association for Counselling and Psychotherapy
1 Regent Place
Rugby CV21 2PJ
Tel: 01788 550899 Fax: 0870 443 5160
www.bac.co.uk

Promotes standards and services in counselling and training, nationally and internationally. Promotes information and advice on all matters related to counselling. It also provides lists of accredited counsellors in local areas.

British Association for Sexual and Relationship Therapy (BASRT)
PO Box 13686
London SW20 9ZH
Tel/fax: 020 8543 2707
www.basrt.org.uk

BASRT is concerned with sexual and relationship function. It provides therapy for couples and accredits counsellors in sexual and relationship work. Members receive Sexual and Relationship Therapy, an international quarterly academic journal.

British Psychological Society
St Andrews House
48 Princess Road East
Leicester LE1 7DR
www.bps.org.uk
Tel: 0116 254 9568 Fax: 0116 247 0787

The British Psychological Society is the UK professional body for psychologists.

Counselling in Primary Care Trust
First Floor, Majestic House
High Street
Staines TW18 4DG
Tel: 01784 441782
www.cpct.co.uk

Promotes, supports and develops counselling psychotherapy and use of counselling skills in primary care.

Counsellors and Psychotherapists in Primary Care
Queensway House
The Queensway
Bognor Regis PO21 1QT
Tel: 01243 870701 Fax: 01243 870702
www.cpc.online.co.uk

Aims to represent counsellors and psychotherapists working in primary care and promote national standards and guidelines for further development and effective counselling throughout NHS primary healthcare.

Royal College of Psychiatrists
17 Belgrave Square
London SW1X 8PG
Tel: 020 7235 2351 Fax: 020 7245 1231
www.rcpsych.ac.uk

The professional and educational body for psychiatrists in the United Kingdom and the Republic of Ireland.

Books

Relationships

Dominian, J. (1995). Marriage, The Definitive Guide to What Makes Marriage Work. London: Heinemann.
Harold, G., Pryor, J. and Reynolds, J. (2001). Not in Front of the Children? How conflict between parents affects children. London: One Plus One.

Mansfield, P. and Collard, J. (1988). The Beginning of the Rest of your Life. London: Macmillan.

Robinson, M. and Smith, D. (1993). Step by Step: Focus on stepfamilies. Hemel Hempstead: Harvester Wheatsheaf.

Adult and infant attachment

Bowlby, J. (1988). A Secure Base: Clinical applications of attachment theory. London: Routledge.

Clulow, C. (Ed.) (2001). Adult Attachment and Couple Psychotherapy: The 'secure base' in practice and research. London: Brunner-Routledge.

Counselling

Burnard, P. (1994). Counselling Skills for Health Professionals (2nd edition). London: Chapman & Hall.

d'Ardenne, P. and Mahtani, A. (1999). Transcultural Counselling in Action (2nd edition). London: Sage.

de Board, R. (1998). Counselling for Toads: A psychological adventure. London: Routledge.

Sexual issues

Bancroft, J. (1989). Human Sexuality and Its Problems (2nd edition). Edinburgh: Churchill Livingstone.

Hawton, K. (1995). Sex Therapy: A practical guide. Oxford: Oxford University Press.

Zilbergeld, B. (1980). Men and Sex. London: Fontana.

Domestic violence

Peckover, S. (2000) Domestic Violence: A framework of good practice. London: CPHVA.

Wykes, T. (1994). Violence and the Health Care Professional. London: Chapman & Hall.

Mental health resources

Grohol, J. (2002). The Insider's Guide to Mental Health Resources Online (2002/2003 edition). New York: Guilford Press.

Murray Parkes, C., Laurgani, P., and Young, B. (Eds.) (1997). Death and Bereavement Across Cultures. London: Routledge.

Norcross, J. et al. (2002). Authoritative Guide to Self-Help Resources in Mental Health. New York: Guilford Press.

All website addresses correct at 1.3.03.

References

Access to Medical Records Act 1990. London: Her Majesty's Stationery Office.

American Psychiatric Association (1994). Diagnostic and Statistical Manual of Mental Disorders (4th edition). Washington, DC: APA.

Andrews, C. and Brown, G. (1988). Marital violence in the community. A biographical approach. British Journal of Psychiatry, 153, 305–12.

Atchley, R. and Miller, S. (1983). Types of elderly couples. In T. Brubaker (Ed.) Family Relationships in Later Life. Beverly Hills. CA: Sage.

Ayles, C. and Reynolds, J. (2001). Identifying and Managing Patients' Relationship Problems in Primary Care: The perspective of health professionals and counsellors. London: One Plus One Marriage and Partnership Research.

Baikie, E. (2002). The impact of dementia on marital relationships. Sexual and Relationship Therapy, 17(3), August, 289–99.

Balakrishna, J. (1998). Sexual abuse: how far do the ripples go? Sexual and Marital Therapy, 13(1), 83–90.

Bancroft, J. (1989). Human Sexuality and its Problems (2nd edition). Edinburgh: Churchill Livingstone.

Barker, C., Pistrang, N., Shapiro, D. and Shaw, I. (1990). Coping and help-seeking in the UK adult population. British Journal of Clinical Psychology, 29, 271–85.

Bayley, J. (2000). Iris: A Memoir. London: Abacus.

Beaumont, G. (1977). Sexual side effects of clomipramine (Anafranil). Journal of International Medical Research, 5, Suppl. 1, 37–44.

Beck, A. (1967). Depression: Clinical, experimental aspects. New York: Harper and Row.

Becker, J., Skinner, L., Abel, G. and Cichon, J. (1986). Levels of post-assault sexual functioning in rape and incest victims. Archives of Sexual Behaviour, 15, 37–49.

Benbow, S. and Jagus, C. (2002). Sexuality in older women with mental health problems. Sexual and Relationship Therapy, 17(3), August, 261–70.

Berardo, F. (1970). Survivorship and social isolation: the case of the aged widower. Family Coordinator, 19, 11–25.

Beresford, B. (1994). Positively Parents: Caring for a severely disabled child. London: Her Majesty's Stationery Office.

Bilney, C. and d'Ardenne, P. (2001). The truth is rarely pure and never simple: a study of some factors affecting history-sharing in the GUM clinic setting. Sexual and Marital Therapy, 16(4), 349–64.

Bloom, B., Asher, S. and White, S. (1978). Marital disruption as a stressor: a review and analysis. Psychological Bulletin, 85, 867–94.

Bowlby, J. (1988). A Secure Base: Clinical applications of attachment theory. London: Routledge.

Brannen, J. and Collard, J. (1982). Marriages in Trouble. The process of seeking help. London: Tavistock Publications.

Bridgewood, A., Lilly, R., Thomas, M., Bacon, J., Sykes, W. and Norris, S. (2000). Living in Britain: Results from the 1998 General Household Survey. London: Office for National Statistics, The Stationery Office, Table 7.1 and 7.2.

British Association for Counselling (1985). Code of Ethics. Rugby: British Association of Counselling.

Brooks, N. and Matson, R (1982). Social-psychological adjustment to multiple sclerosis. Social Science and Medicine, 16, 2129–35.

Brown, G.W. and Harris, T. (1978). Social Origins of Depression: A study of psychiatric disorder in women. London: Tavistock.

Burnard, P. (1994). Counselling Skills for Health Professionals (2nd edition). London: Chapman & Hall.

Butler, M. and Clarke, J. (1991). Couple therapy with homosexual men. In D. Hooper and W. Dryden (Eds.) Couple Therapy: A handbook. Milton Keynes: Open University Press, 196–206.

Calmen, K. (1984). Quality of life in cancer patients: an hypothesis. Journal of Medical Ethics, 10, 124–7.

Cappelli, M., McGrath, P., Daniels, T., Manion, I. and Schillinger, J. (1994). Marital quality of parents of children with spina-bifida – a case-comparison study. Journal of Developmental and Behavioral Pediatrics, 15(5) October, 320–6.

Carpenter, B. and Herbert, E. (1994). The peripheral parent: research issues and reflections on the role of fathers in early intervention. PMDL Link, 19, Summer.

Champion, L. (2000). Depression. In L. Champion and M. Power (Eds.) Adult Psychological Problems, 2nd Edition. Hove: Psychology Press.

Clulow, C. (Ed.) (2001). Adult Attachment and Couple Psychotherapy – the 'secure base' in practice and research. London: Brunner-Routledge.

Clulow, C. and Mattinson, J. (1989). Marriage Inside Out. Harmondsworth: Penguin Books.

Community Care Act 1990. London: Her Majesty's Stationery Office.

Cooper, C., Sloan, S. and Williams, S. (1988). Occupational Stress Indicator Management Guide. Windsor: NFER. Nelson.

Corney, R. (1998). Evaluation of The Brief Encounters Training Course. London: University of Greenwich.

Cowan, C. and Cowan, P. (1992). When Partners Become Parents: The big life changes for couples. New York: Basic Books.

Coyne, J. and Downey, G. (1991). Social factors and psychopathology: stress, social support, and coping processes. Annual Review of Psychology, 42, 401–25.

Coyne, J., Ellard, J. and Smith, D. (1990). Social support, interdependence, and the dilemmas of helping. In B. Sarason, I. Sarason and G. Pierce (Eds.) Social Support: An interactional view. New York: John Wiley, 129–49.

CPHVA (Community Practitioners' and Health Visitors' Association) (1998). Domestic Violence: The role of the community nurse. London: CPHVA.

CPHVA (Community Practitioners' and Health Visitors' Association) (2001). Postnatal Depression and Maternal Mental Health, a Public Health Priority. London: CPHVA.

Crowe, M. and Ridley, J. (1990). Therapy with Couples: A behavioural-systems approach to marital and sexual problems. Oxford: Blackwell Scientific Publications.

Cudmore, L. and Judd, D. (2001). Traumatic loss and the couple. In C. Clulow (Ed.) Adult Attachment and Couple Psychotherapy – The 'secure base' in practice and research. Hove: Brunner-Routledge.

Cutrona, A. (1996). Social Support in Couples. Thousand Oaks, CA: Sage.

D'Ardenne, P. (1988). Sexual dysfunction in a transcultural setting. In M. Cole and W. Dryden (Eds.) Sex Therapy in Britain. Milton Keynes: Open University Press.

D'Ardenne, P. (1999). The sexual and relationship needs of gay and lesbian people. Sexual and Marital Therapy, 14(1), 5–8.

D'Ardenne, P. and Balakrishna, J. (2001). Domestic violence and intimacy: what the relationship therapist needs to know. Sexual and Marital Therapy, 16(3), 229–46.

D'Ardenne, P. and Mahtani, A. (1999). Transcultural Counselling in Action (2nd edition). London: Sage.

D'Ardenne, P. and McCann, E. (1997). The sexual and relationship needs of people with psychosis – a neglected topic. Sexual and Marital Therapy, 12(4), 301–3.

D'Ardenne, P., Estreich, S., Forster, G. and Goh Ben, B. (1990). The assessment of a clinical psychology service in an East London sexually transmitted diseases clinic. Sexual and Marital Therapy, 5(1), 55–62.

De Board, R. (1998). Counselling for Toads: A psychological adventure. London: Routledge.

De Silva, P. (1999). Sexual consequences of non-sexual trauma. Sexual and Marital Therapy, 14(2), 143–50.

De Silva, P. (2001). Impact of trauma on sexual functioning and sexual relationships. Sexual and Marital Therapy, 16(3), 269–78.

Department of Health (1992). Health of the Nation. London: Her Majesty's Stationery Office.

Department of Health (1999). Making a Difference: Strengthening the nursing, midwifery and health visiting contribution to health and healthcare. London: Her Majesty's Stationery Office.

Dominelli, L. (1988). Anti-Racist Social Work. London: Macmillan Education.

Dominian, J. (1995). Marriage: The definitive guide to what makes marriage work. London: Heinemann.

Dowrick, C. (1992). Improving mental health through primary care. British Journal of General Practice, 42, 382–6.

Duck, S. (1991). Friends for Life. Hemel Hempstead: Harvester Wheatsheaf.

Duck, S. (1998). Human Relationships (3rd edition). London: Sage.

Dupont, S. (1996). Sexual function and ways of coping in patients with multiple sclerosis and their partners. Sexual and Marital Therapy, 11(4), 359–72.

Ehlers, A. and Clark, D. (2000). A cognitive theory of post-traumatic stress disorder. Behaviour Research and Therapy, 38, 319–45.

Fairburn, C. and Cooper, P. (1996). In K. Hawton, P. Salkovskis, J. Kirk and D. Clarke (Eds.) Cognitive Behaviour Therapy for Psychiatric Problems: A practical guide. Oxford: Oxford: Medical Publications, pp. 277–314.

Falloon, I. and Lieberman, R. (1983). Behavioural family interventions in the management of chronic schizophrenia. In W. McFarlane (Ed.) Family Therapy in Schizophrenia. New York: Guilford Press.

Falloon, I., Boyd, J. and McGill, C. (1984). Family Care of Schizophrenia. London: Guilford Press.

Fennell, M. (1989). Depression. In K. Howlan, P. Salkovskis, J. Kirk, and D. Clark (Eds.) Cognitive Behaviour Therapy for Psychiatric Problems. Oxford: Oxford University Press.

Faulkner, A. (1997). Knowing Our Own Minds: A survey of how people with emotional distress take care of their lives. London: Mental Health Foundation.

Ferri, K. and Smith, K. (1996). Parenting in the 1990s. London: Family Policy Study Centre.

Fieldman-Summers, C., Gordon, P. and Maegher, J. (1979). The impact of rape on sexual satisfaction. Journal of Abnormal Psychology, 88, 101–5.

Freud, S. (1900). The Interpretation of Dreams. London: Hogarth Press.

Gelles, R. (1995). Contemporary Families: A sociological view. Thousand Oaks, CA: Sage.

Gilhooly, M., Sweeting, H., Whittick, J. and McKee, K. (1994). Family care of the dementing elderly. International Review of Psychiatry, 6, 29–40.

Goddard, E. and Savage, D. (1994). The General Household Survey 1991. Supplement A: People aged 65 and over. London: Office for National Statistics, The Stationery Office.

Greene, B. (1994). Ethnic minority lesbian and gay men: mental health and treatment issues. Journal of Consulting and Clinical Psychology, April.

Grimer, M. (1987). Making Marriage Work. London: Geoffrey Chapman.

Grohol, J. (2002). The Insider's Guide to Mental Health Resources Online. New York: Guilford Press.

Hall, R. and Simmonds, W. (1973). The POW wife: a psychiatric appraisal. Archives of General Psychiatry, 29, 690–4.

Harland, R. and Huws, R. (1997). Sexual problems in diabetes and the role of psychological intervention. Sexual and Marital Therapy, 12(2), 147–57.

Harold, G., Pryor, J. and Reynolds, J. (2001). Not in Front of the Children. London: One Plus One Marriage and Partnership Research.

Hawton, K. (1984). Sexual adjustment of men who have had strokes. Journal of Psychosomatic Research, 28, 243–9.

Hawton, K. (1985). Sex Therapy: A practical guide. Oxford: Oxford Medical Publications.

Hendryx, M., Doebbeling, B. and Kearns, D. (1994). Mental health treatment in primary care: physician treatment choices and psychiatric admission rates. Family Practice Research Journal, 14, 127–37.

Herbert, E. and Carpenter, B. (1994). Fathers: the secondary partners: professional perceptions and a father's reflections. Children and Society, 8(1) 31–41.

Hillard, P. (1985). Physical abuse in pregnancy. Obstetrics and Gynaecology, 66, 185–90.

Holmshaw, J. and Hillier, S. (2000). Gender and culture: a sociological perspective to mental health problems in women. In D. Kohen (Ed.) Women and Mental Health. London: Routledge.

Home Office (2000). Reducing Domestic Violence . . . What Works? Briefing Notes. London: PRC Unit Publications.

Hooper, D. and. Dryden, W. (Eds.) (1991). Couple Therapy: A handbook. Milton Keynes: Open University Press.

Hughes, T. (1998). Birthday Letters, London: Faber and Faber.

Huish, M., Kumar, D. and Stones, C. (1998). Stoma surgery and sexual problems in ostomates. Sexual and Marital Therapy, 13(3), 311–28.

Ievers, C. and Drotar, D. (1996). Family and parental functioning in cystic fibrosis. Journal of Developmental and Behavioral Pediatrics, 17(1), February, 48–55.

Jacobson, B. (1994). Health in the East End – Annual public health report. London: East London and the City Health Authority and City and East London FHSA.

Jarman, B. (1992). Predicting psychiatric admission rates. British Medical Journal, 304, 1146–51.

Kaplan, H. (1990). Sex, intimacy and the aging process. Journal of the American Academy of Psychoanalysis, 18, 185–205.

Kaplan, H. (1992). Comprehensive Textbook of Psychiatry. Baltimore, MD: Williams and Wilkins.

Kendell, R. and Zealley, A. (1992). Companion to Psychiatric Studies (4th edition). London: Churchill Livingstone.

Kershaw, C., Bidd, T., Kinshott, G., Mattinson, G., Mayhew, P. and Myhill, A. (2000). The 2000 British Crime Survey. London: Home Office Statistical Bulletin.

Kitzinger, S. (1980). Pregnancy and Childbirth. London: Michael Joseph.

Kohen, D. (2000). Perinatal psychiatry. In D. Kohen (Ed.) Women and Mental Health. London: Routledge.

Kolodny, R., Masters, W. and Johnson, V. (1979). Textbook of Sexual Medicine. Boston: Little, Brown.

Kravetz, S., Gross, Y., Weiler, B., Ben-Yakar, M., Tadir, M. and Stern, M. (1995). Self-concept, marital vulnerability and brain damage. Brain Injury, 9(2), 131–9.

Krupnick, J., Green, B. and Miranda, J. (1998). Group interpersonal psychotherapy for the treatment of PTSD following interpersonal trauma. Paper presented at the Annual Meeting of the Society for Psychotherapy Research. Snowbird. UT. June.

Leboyer, F. (1977). Birth without Violence. London: Fontana.

Leff, J. and Vaughan, C. (1981). The role of maintenance therapy and relatives' expressed emotion in relapse of schizophrenia: a two year follow up. British Journal of Psychiatry, 139, 102–34.

Lego, C. and Thompson, J. (1996). Race, Culture and Counselling. Buckingham: Open University Press.

Levenson, R., Carstenson, L. and Gottman, J. (1993). Long term marriage: age, gender, and satisfaction. Psychology and Aging, 8, 301–13.

Littlewood, R. and Lipsedge, M. (1997). Aliens and Alienists: Ethnic minorities and psychiatry (3rd edition). London: Unwin Hyman.

Lyons, R. and Meade, A. (1995). Painting a new face on relationships: relationship remodelling in response to chronic illness. In S. Duck and J. Wood (Eds.) Confronting Relationship Challenges. Thousand Oaks, CA: Sage.

Mansfield, P. and Collard, J. (1988). The Beginning of the Rest of Your Life. London: Macmillan.

McAllister, F. (Ed.) (1995). Marital Breakdown and The Health of the Nation (2nd edition). London: One Plus One Marriage and Partnership Research.

McCann, E. (1994). The expression of sexuality in clients with enduring mental health problems. Unpublished MSc Thesis, University of London

McCubbin, H., Hunter, E. and Dahl, B. (1975). Residuals of war: families of prisoners of war and servicemen missing in action. Journal of Social Issues, 31, 95–109.

McCulloch, D., Young, R., Prescott, R., Campbell, R. and Clarke, B. (1984). The natural history of impotence in diabetic men. Diabetologia, 26, 437–40.

McFarlane, A. and Bookless, C. (2001). The effect of PTSD on interpersonal relationships: issues for emergency service workers. Sexual and Marital Therapy, 16(3), 261–8.

McFarlane, A. and van der Kolk, B. (1996). Trauma and its challenge to society, in A.B. van der Kolk and A. McFarlane, Traumatic Stress – the effects of overwhelming experience on the mind, body and society. New York: Guilford Press.

McFarlane J., Parker, B., Soeken, K. and Bullock, L. (1992). Assessing for abuse during pregnancy. Journal of the American Medical Association, 267, 3176–8.

McKenna, S. and Hunt, S. (1994). A measure of family disruption for use in chickenpox and other childhood illnesses. Social Science and Medicine, 38(5), March, 725–31.

Mezey, G. and Bewley, S. (1997). Domestic violence and pregnancy. British Medical Journal, 314, May, 1295.

Midence, K. (1994). The effects of chronic illness on children and their families – an overview. Genetic Social and General Psychology Monographs, 120(3), August, 311–26.

Mills, B. (2001). Impact of trauma on sexuality and relationships. Sexual and Marital Therapy, 16(3), 197–205.

Mills, B. and Turnbull, G. (2001). After trauma: why assessment of intimacy should be an integral part of medico-legal reports. Sexual and Marital Therapy, 16(3), 299–308

Mirlees-Black, C. (1999). Domestic Violence: Findings from a New British Crime Survey self-completion questionnaire. London: Home Office, Research Study 191.

Mooney, A. and Statham, J. (2002). The Pivot Generation: Informal care and work after fifty. Abingdon: The Foundation by the Policy Press.

Morrod, D. (2002). Brief Encounters Training Manual. London: One Plus One. Marriage and Partnership Research.

Murray, L. and Andrews, L. (2000). The Social Baby: Understanding babies' communication from birth. Richmond: CP Publishing.

Murray, L., Sinclair, D. Cooper, P., Ducournan, P., Turner, P. and Stein, A. (1999). The socioemotional development of 5-year-old children of postnatally depressed mothers. Child Psychology and Psychiatry, 40(8), November, 1259–71.

Murray Parkes, C. (1986). Bereavement. Studies of Grief in Adult Life (2nd edition). London: Tavistock Publications.

Nazroo, J. (1999). Ethnicity and Mental Health: Findings from a National Community Survey, London: Policy Studies Institute.

Nichols, K. (1991). Counselling and renal failure, in H. Davis and L. Fallowfield (Eds.) Counselling and Communication in Health Care. Chichester: John Wiley.

Norcross, J. et al. (2000). Authoritative Guide to Self-help Resources in Mental Health. New York: The Guilford Press.

Oakley, A. (1988). Is social support good for the health of mothers and babies? Journal of Infant and Reproductive Psychology, 6, 3–21.

Oakley, A., Rigby, S. and Hickey, D. (1994). Life stress and class inequality: explaining the health of women and children. European Journal of Public Health, 4, 81–91.

O'Connell, M., Leburg, E. and Donaldson, C. (1990). Working with Sex Offenders: Guidelines for therapist selection. Newbury Park, CA: Sage.

Oddy, M. (2001). Sexual relationships following brain injury. Sexual and Marital Therapy, 16(3), 247–59.

Office for National Statistics (2000). Marriage, Divorce and Adoption Statistics 2000. Series FM2, no. 28, p. 76. London: HMSO.

O'Hara, M. and Swain, A. (1996). Rates and risks of postpartum depression: a meta-analysis. International Review of Psychiatry 8(1), 37–54.

Oliviere, D., Hargreaves, R. and Monroe, B. (1998). Good Practices in Paliative Care: A psychosocial perspective. Aldershot: Ashgate.

One Plus One (1998). Marriages in later life. Bulletin Plus, 2 (3).

One Plus One (2001). Briefing Notes for Encounters with Families. London: One Plus One.

One Plus One (2002). Involved fathers or father figures are key for children. Bulletin Plus, 6(2).

Oxman, A., Scott, E., Sellors, J., Clarke, J., Millson, M., Rasooly, I, Frank, J., Naus, M. and Goldblatt, E (1994). Partner notification for sexually transmitted diseases: an overview of the evidence. Canadian Journal of Public Health, 85, S41–47.

Pahl, J. (1982). Men who assault their wives – what can health visitors do to help? Health Visitor, 55, 528–30.

Palmer, S. and Laungani, P. (Eds.) (1999). Counselling in a Multicultural Society. London: Sage.

Parad, H. and Parad, L. (Eds.) (1990). Crisis Intervention Book 2: The practitioner's sourcebook for brief therapy. Milwaukee, WI: Family Service America.

Paykel, E., Emms, E., Fletcher, J. and Rassaby, E. (1980). Life events and social support in puerperal depression. British Journal of Psychiatry, 136, 339–46.

Peckover, S. (2000). Domestic Violence: A framework for good practice. London: CPHVA.

Phanjoo, A. (2002). Sex and intimacy in older people. Sexual and Relationship Therapy, 17(3), August, 229–30.

Power-Smith, P. (1991). Problems in older people's longer term sexual relationships. Sexual and Marital Therapy, 6(3), 287–96.

Priebe, S., Oliver, J. and Kaiser, W. (Eds.) (1999). Quality of Life and Mental Health Care. Petersfield: Wrightson Biomedical Publishers.

Proctor, B. and Inskipp, F. (1993). Skills for Supervising and Being Supervised. Audiotape and Booklets. Tape 1: Being Supervised. St Leonards on Sea: Alexia Publications.

Revenson, T. and Majerovitz, S. (1991). The effects of chronic illness on the spouse. Arthritis Care and Research, 4, 63–72.

Reynolds, J. (Ed.) (2001). Not in Front of the Children? How conflict between parents affects children. London: One Plus One Marriage and Partnership Research.

Robinson, M. and Smith, D. (1993). Step by Step: Focus on stepfamilies. Hemel Hempstead: Harvester Wheatsheaf.

Rogers, A., Pilgrim, D. and Latham, M. (1996). Understanding and promoting mental health. A study of familial views. London: Health Education Authority, Family Research Reports.

Ross, H. and Hardy, G. (1999). GP referrals to adult psychological services: a research agenda for promoting needs-led practice through the involvement of mental health clinicians. Journal of Medical Psychology, 72, 75–91.

Roy. A. (1987). Five risk factors for depression. British Journal of Psychiatry, 150, 536–41.

Royal College of Nursing (2002). Nurse Practitioners – an RCN guide to the nurse practitioner role, competencies and programme accreditation. London: RCN.

Rusbult, C. and Buunk, A. (1993). Commitment processes in close relationships: an interdependence analysis. Journal of Social and Personal Relationships, 10, 175–203.

Sage, L. (2001). Bad Blood. London: Fourth Estate.

Sanders, M., Nicholson, J. and Floyd, F. (1997). Couples' relationships and children. In W.K. Halford and H.J. Markman (Eds.) Clinical Handbook of Marriage and Couples Interventions. Chichester: Wiley.

SANE (2000). Campaign poster. London.

Scholte op Reimer, W., de Haan, R., Pijnenborg, J., Limbourg, M. and van des Bos, G. (1998). Assessment of burden in partners of stroke patients with the sense of competence questionnaire. Stroke, 29, 373–9.

Schone, B. and Weinick, R. (1998). Health-related behaviours and the benefits of marriage for elderly persons. Gerontologist, 38(5), 618–27.

Schroeder, T. (1997). Couples counselling. In S. Palmer and G. McMahon (Eds.) Handbook of Counselling (2nd edition). London: Routledge.

Scott, M. (1997). Counselling for trauma and post-traumatic stress disorder. In S. Palmer and G. McMahon (Eds.) Handbook of Counselling (2nd edition). London: Routledge.

Seigal, J. (1997). Counselling people with disabilities/chronic illnesses. In S. Palmer and G. McMahon (Eds.) Handbook of Counselling (2nd edition). London: Routledge.

SHASTD (1993). Partner Notification Guidelines. London: Society of Health Advisors in Sexually Transmitted Diseases.

Shipton, G. (Ed.) (1997). Supervision of Psychotherapy and Counselling – Making a place to think. Buckingham: Open University Press.

Simons, J. (Ed.) (1999). High Divorce Rates: The state of the evidence on reasons and remedies. Research Series No. 2/99 (Vol. 1). London: Lord Chancellor's Department.

Simons, J., Reynolds, J. and Morison, L. (2001). Randomised controlled trial of training health visitors to identify and help couples with relationship problems following a birth. British Journal of General Practice, October, 793–9.

Simons, S. (1991). Couple therapy with lesbians. In D. Cooper and W. Dryden (Eds.) Couple Therapy: A handbook. Milton Keynes: Open University Press.

Smith, R. (1997). Mixed-HIV status couples: navigating the challenges of everyday life. Body Positive, XI(3), October.

Social Trends (1999). Social Focus on Older People. London: The Stationery Office.

Social Trends (2000). A Hundred Years of Social Change. London: The Stationery Office.

Statistics Canada (1993). Violence against Women Survey: Survey highlights. Canada: Statistics Canada.

Stephens, M. and Clark, S. (1997). Reciprocity in the expression of emotional support among later-life couples coping with stroke. In B. Gottlieb (Ed.) Coping with Chronic Stress. New York: Plenum Press.

Sutton, C. (1997). Counselling in the personal social services, in S. Palmer and G. McMahon (Eds.) Handbook of Counselling (2nd edition). London: Routledge.

Sweet, B. and Cape, I. (1976). Obstetric Care. Aylesbury: HM+M Publishers.

Truax, C. and Carkuff, R. (1967). Towards Effective Counseling and Psychotherapy. Chicago: Aldine.

Trudel, G., Turgeon, L. and Piche, L. (2000). Marital and sexual aspects of old age. Sexual and Marital Therapy, 15(4), 381–405.

Ustun, T. and Gater, R. (1994). Integrating mental health into primary care. Current Opinions in Psychiatry, 7, 173–80.

van der Kolk, A. and McFarlane, A. (1996). Traumatic Stress – The effects of overwhelming experience on the mind, body and society. New York: Guilford Press.

Weeks, D. (2002). Sex for the mature adult: health, self-esteem and countering ageist stereotypes. Sexual and Relationship Therapy, 17(3), 231–40.

Weeks, D. and James, J. (1998). Secrets of the Superyoung. New York: Villard.

Weijmar Schultz, W., Bransfield, D., van der Viel, H. and Bouma, J. (1992). Sexual outcome following female genital cancer treatment: a critical review of methods of investigation and results. Sexual and Marital Therapy, 7(1), 29–64.

Weiss, R. and Aved, B. (1978). Marital satisfaction and depression as predictors of physical health status. Journal of Consulting and Clinical Psychology, 46, 1379–84.

Werlinich, C. (2001). Dealing with the violent loss of a child. Family Focus, Issue FF12, Minneapolis: National Council on Family Relations.

Wikler, L. (1986). Periodic stresses of older mentally retarded children: an exploratory study. American Journal of Mental Deficiency, 90, 703–6.

Williams, H. (1972). True Resurrection. London: Fount Paperbacks.

Williams, M. (1998). Gender and sexuality. In D. Oliviere, R. Hargreaves and B. Monroe (Eds.) Good Practices in Palliative Care: A psychosocial perspective. Aldershot: Ashgate.

Woods, R. (2001). Discovering the person with Alzheimer's disease: cognitive, emotional and behavioural aspects. Aging and Mental Health, 5, Suppl.1, S7–S16.

Wright, D. and Aquilino, W. (1998). Influence of emotional support exchange in marriage on caregiving wives' burden and marital satisfaction. Family Relations, 47(2), 195–204.

Wright, R. (1993). Alzheimer's Disease and Marriage. London: Sage Publications.

Wykes, T. (1994). Violence and the Health Care Professional. London: Chapman & Hall.

Young, B. and Papadatou, D. (1997). Childhood death and bereavement across cultures, Chapter 10 in C. Murray-Parkes, P. Laungani and B. Young (Eds.) Death and Bereavement Across Cultures. London: Routledge.

Zeiba, A., Dudek, D. and Jawor, M. (1997). Marital functioning in patients with major depression. Sexual and Marital Therapy, 12(4), November, 313–20.

Zilbergeld, B. (1980). Men and Sex. London: Fontana.

Index